The Spirit-Driven Leader

Other Books by Carnegie Samuel Calian

Today's Pastor in Tomorrow's World (rev. ed.)

The Significance of Eschatology

In the Thoughts of Nicolas Berdyaev

Berdyaev's Philosophy of Hope (rev. ed.)

Icon and Pulpit: The Protestant-Orthodox Encounter

*Grace, Guts and Goods: How to Stay Christian
in an Affluent Society*

The Gospel according to the Wall Street Journal

For All Your Seasons: Biblical Directions through Life's Passages

Where's the Passion for Excellence in the Church?

*Theology without Boundaries: Encounters of Eastern Orthodoxy
and Western Tradition*
(translated also in Korean)

Survival or Revival: Ten Keys to Church Vitality
(translated also in Korean)

The Ideal Seminary: Pursuing Excellence in Theological Education

The Spirit-Driven Leader

Seven Keys to Succeeding under Pressure

Carnegie Samuel Calian

to
Jeanne Sullivan
I know how much
Jill & Philip appreciate
you and your husband
Joe's mentorship to you son.
May God's grace
be with you.
Doris & Sam
Calian
7/12/2010

WJK WESTMINSTER
JOHN KNOX PRESS
LOUISVILLE · KENTUCKY

First edition
Published by Westminster John Knox Press
Louisville, Kentucky

10 11 12 13 14 15 16 17 18 19—10 9 8 7 6 5 4 3 2 1

Book design by Drew Stevens
Cover design by designpointinc.com

Library of Congress Cataloging-in-Publication Data

Calian, Carnegie Samuel.
  The spirit-driven leader : seven keys to succeeding under pressure / by Carnegie Samuel Calian.
    p. cm.
  Includes bibliographical references.
  ISBN 978-0-664-22986-3 (alk. paper)
  1. Leadership—Religious aspects—Christianity.   2. Success—Religious aspects—Christianity.
I. Title.
  BV4597.53.L43C35   2010
  253'.2—dc22
                                                                      2010003748

PRINTED IN THE UNITED STATES OF AMERICA

∞ The paper used in this publication meets the minimum requirements
of the American National Standard for Information Sciences—Permanence
of Paper for Printed Library Materials, ANSI Z39.48-1992

Westminster John Knox Press advocates the responsible use of our natural resources.
The text paper of this book is made from 30% post-consumer waste.

This book is dedicated to my wife, Doris, on our fiftieth anniversary
(2009) and to our three wonderful families
of grandchildren and their parents.

Lois and Dennis Trautvetter
Rachel
Paula
Caleb

Jill and Philip Calian
Luke
Sam
Christian
Julian

Sara and Raffi Kaprielian
Thomas
Grace
Hannah

And to my sister, Elizabeth Calian,
a devoted teacher for thirty years to children.

Contents

Part 2: Ways Organizations Build Community

Acknowledgments

I am grateful to so many sources that aided me in this modest volume—materials researched from travels and interviews; books and articles; numerous discussions among many followers and leaders of organizations, profit and nonprofit; and the opportunities to teach and lecture in a number of institutions of higher education at home and abroad, which also included graduate schools of business, an experience that I found instructional and useful. All these encounters have been learning opportunities highlighting the many intersections and conflicts that occur in business, education, health care, and religious institutions in today's diverse and complex marketplace.

My special thanks to the librarians who have made available resources throughout my study in completing this project. I especially appreciated the use of the libraries at Oxford University as well as the warm welcome my wife and I received at Harris Manchester College from Principal Ralph Waller, his faculty colleagues, and his administrative staff. I was invited to join them as a senior academic fellow for the spring term of 2006. I am grateful to the college librarian, Susan Kellerman, for her generous support in securing material and providing study space for my research. My gratitude for Oxford also includes the opportunity to attend classes and enriching programs; in my case, this led to the discovery of the Said Graduate School of Business with its Jeffrey Skoll Center for Social Entrepreneurship, which I found informative and helpful.

I am thankful for the assistance of Betsy Hawley in the early stages of preparation of the manuscript and to the faithful members of the Barbour Library at Pittsburgh Theological Seminary for their unfailing encouragement throughout my writing project—especially Anita Johnson. And my appreciation for the invitations from Dean Kenneth Dunn, at the Tepper Graduate School of Business at Carnegie Mellon University, and Dean John Delaney, at the Katz Graduate School of Business at the University of Pittsburgh, and to their faculty colleagues and administrative staff for their generous support and encouragement, including access to the resources in their fine institutions.

My heartfelt thanks also to members of my family for their encouragement and comments as I completed this project following my recovery from a car accident with eight broken ribs. I will be ever grateful to my loving wife, Doris, for her spirit of commitment and for the fun and adventure we continue to have together. She is my favorite critic and friend, with her many gifted talents. Together we are both indebted to God's gift of our family and the divine grace that enriches our lives daily.

Finally, I would be remiss if I didn't also express my debt to the executive editor of Westminster John Knox Press, Stephanie Egnotovich, for her editorial leadership and support on this and previous writing projects. Stephanie's wisdom and encouragement are truly missed with her untimely death. I am also grateful to the editorial director of Westminster John Knox Press, David Dobson, for continuing in Stephanie's absence and to his devoted staff for the completion of this publication process. Last but not least, my special thanks to Jim Davidson for interviewing me for the introduction to this volume and for his insightful comments in reading drafts from his dual perspective as a reporter/editor, his first career, and as a Presbyterian pastor in Elizabeth, Pennsylvania, near Pittsburgh. In concluding these acknowledgments, I do take responsibility for the contents of this book.

Carnegie Samuel Calian
Pittsburgh, Pennsylvania

Introduction to Author and Book

Sometimes we find life-changing advice in unlikely places. That was the case with Brad Anderson, the CEO of the electronics retailer Best Buy, who told his story to *Fortune*. Anderson, the son of a Lutheran minister, briefly attended seminary, which he credited as "by far the best leadership preparation I received." Anderson recalled his course in preaching: "The professor told us something that affected me deeply: He said that each of us would be lucky if we had one good sermon to give, and that it could take us years to find it. I found that idea to be intimidating, and I left the seminary not long afterward—without a sermon."

Anderson applied the lesson thirty-one years later when the founder of Best Buy was choosing a successor. "I did something that day that was completely out of character," Anderson said. "I told him he should pick me. It had taken thirty-one years, but I finally realized at that moment what my one good sermon was—I could explain why I saw myself as a leader."

Carnegie Samuel Calian has written a variety of books about seminary education and other topics. Since his 2006 retirement as president of Pittsburgh Theological Seminary, he has also been refining his ideas on organizational behavior and marketplace ethics into "one good sermon" that he delivers here, drawing on his recent teaching, lecturing, reading, and thinking as he served as a guest professor and visiting scholar in business schools at Oxford University, Carnegie Mellon University, and the University of Pittsburgh.

The Spirit-Driven Leader dispenses practical advice for leaders and followers in organizations of all types, with special words for those who find themselves at odds with others in their organization. Dr. Calian tells stories about things going awry within an organization, and he explains how leaders can work to resolve conflict and inspire hope. The book is organized into seven chapters, each focused on a key element in leadership: creativity, competence, commitment, character, collegiality, compassion, and courage.

One thing you should know about the author's background is that he served for twenty-five years as president of Pittsburgh Theological Seminary before retiring in 2006. This means he learned about leadership not by studying it, observing it, or speculating about it, but by practicing it over the long haul. On the seminary's organizational chart, the two-way arrows connected his office not just with faculty, students, and staff, but also to churches and their pastors, to trustees, to donors, to businesses, to educators and other professionals, to civic leaders and government agencies, and to the seminary's neighbors in the Highland Park and Oakland neighborhoods of Pittsburgh.

With such an array of people to please—or to offend—it's no wonder that presidents don't last long in institutions of higher learning. According to one recent calculation, a new president of a major research university can expect a going-away party within five years or less. Leaders wear down and often wear out their welcomes. Many prove too ill-fitted to the job at hand. Some run into palace revolts, as one constituency or another conspires to place one of its own in the president's chair.

Seminary presidents generally serve longer than university presidents, yet few can match Dr. Calian's tenure on the job. To understand how he did it, you need to read between the lines. This book, like his 2002 book *The Ideal Seminary*, is not a personal memoir, nor is it a cookbook full of recipes for leadership. In seeking to bridge the divide between leaders and followers, Dr. Calian favors organizations that get things done without a top-down leader barking out every order. "There has to be teamwork," he told me in one of our conservations while he was writing this book. "The key is empowering others, and that's why I see leadership as followership and followership as leadership." He urges leaders to help others "articulate what they're thinking." This approach is evident in the advice he says he once gave to the chair of a successful search committee: "You lead, and let me know how things are going."

The book calls people within organizations to stretch their current way of doing things in order to become more collegial, more sensitive to others, more creative, and more receptive to what Dr. Calian calls "uncommon sense" as an alternative to the rote common-sense approach that often leads nowhere. His advice is meant for leaders and followers of all organizations—large and small, nonprofit and for-profit, secular and ecclesiastical, churched and unchurched. In a word, his approach is pastoral. It comes from the heart, with faith, hope, and charity toward those inside and outside the organization.

"The debate we should be having in religious and educational institutions today," Dr. Calian says, "is how can the church and school have a new outlook on increasing the ways and means of their service to the world? How can we save the world when we are so occupied with saving our own structures?"

In a time of economic turbulence, that's good advice for leaders and followers in all kinds of organizations. "The end point is to build trust," Dr. Calian says. "If you don't build trust, you don't get anyone to go with you."

Here, in brief, are the topics considered in the seven chapters of this book:

Creativity: Urging leaders to "see solutions where others see barriers," the author explains that an organization's creative vision is not just the product of one person. Vision may begin with people like Bill and Melinda Gates, Costco's Jim Sinegal, or News Corp.'s Rupert Murdoch, but nothing will happen unless others recognize the vision and take the risk of discerning its possibilities.

Competence: "You're much better than you think you are," Dr. Calian writes, noting how organizations often fail to utilize the gifts and graces of their people. The chapter tells the story of Wendy Kopp, who founded Teach for America to put the talents of college graduates to use as public school teachers. The chapter also explores lifelong learning and career development projects undertaken by successful organizations.

Commitment: Using examples that include Lee Iacocca, King Solomon, and Enron whistle-blower Sherron Watkins, the chapter insists on honesty and integrity as the core of leadership and followership, both of which the author describes as "spiritual callings." The chapter discusses how to distinguish skirmishes from battles and delves into the issue of executive compensation.

Character: Add confidence and humility and what do you get? Credibility. Dr. Calian starts with Abraham Lincoln to show how successful leaders listen to human needs and earn the trust of others. Humility is not just understanding your own limitations, but the limitations of others as well. "Living with imperfect persons" describes life in any organization.

Collegiality: The rise of the Pittsburgh Steelers and the Johnsonville Sausage Co. both demonstrate how an organization can prosper when its people affirm one another's strength and value. Dr. Calian explains how Johnsonville CEO Ralph Stayer went from a top-down authority figure to a player/coach who championed on-the-job learning. The chapter also describes how a commitment to "dialogue" can mask deep division if the dialogue consists of "superficial discussions to trade biases."

Compassion: Pointing out that the Golden Rule ("Do unto others . . .") is core wisdom in every religious tradition, Dr. Calian explains how it is also a core business value. He also turns to the topic of compassion as he tells the story of growing up in Los Angeles as a child of first-generation Armenian immigrants, and the chapter takes compassion into the business arena with "Ten Strategic Guidelines for the Marketplace."

Courage: In a wide-ranging final chapter, the illustrations range from David and Goliath to Pakistani attorney Asma Jahangir, polar explorer Ernest Shackleton, and Abraham Lincoln's "Meditation on the Divine Will." Here the author also shares his appreciation for Kent M. Keith's understanding of paradox, which Dr. Calian refers to as "uncommon sense," an ability to think outside the framework of common sense.

Taken together, the chapters call on us all to be more inclusive in understanding what it means to lead and to follow. Doing that takes a largeness of spirit on the part of both leaders and followers, Dr. Calian explains. The ABCs of everyone's call are nothing less than to "pull together to have a more fulfilling life."

Jim Davidson
Elizabeth, Pennsylvania

PART ONE

Leadership that Inspires Hope:
Creativity,
Competence,
Commitment,
Character

1
Creativity

Recently, I was teaching a class at Carnegie Mellon University's Academy for Lifelong Learning titled "The Gospel According to the *Wall Street Journal* in a Changing World."[1] The course centered on the values and ethics of our global society as reflected in the pages of the *Wall Street Journal*. The class discussions were especially timely due to the announcement that media mogul Rupert Murdoch had publicly offered five-billion-plus dollars to purchase the *Journal*. His offering price was regarded as generous, given the stock price at the time.

What received media attention far more than the price tag were Murdoch's leadership style and intention to own this world-renowned newspaper. His character and ideological interests were being questioned. What were his true motives? Would he undermine the *Journal*'s integrity? A leader's character and creativity play a significant role in determining whether leadership matters and merits respect both inside and outside of an organization. Murdoch had a strong desire to project a positive image of himself as the principal shareholder and CEO of the news corporation. He believed his company had the resources to revitalize the *Journal* financially and to enlarge its market share of readers. Besides, he was eager to add its reputation to "Rupert's World" of companies, which already included the Fox Network (television, cable, and satellite operations); his film entertainment assets; many newspapers (including the *New York Post*, the *Times* of London, and his Australian papers); magazines; book publishing interests (including HarperCollins); and

Internet assets (MySpace, etc.). His holdings indicate his creative spirit at work and his high energy, which helped him to transcend his modest beginnings in Australia.

Time magazine, in a front-page story, referred to him as "The Last Tycoon" of the media industry within our changing world.[2] Nevertheless, the Bancroft family, principal owner of the Dow Jones Co., including its prize *Journal,* was at first not convinced that Murdoch was the right buyer. His character was an issue in spite of his creative accomplishments. Murdoch and his associates worked hard to change the mind-set of the Bancroft family and also spent time interacting with the *Journal*'s editors, reporters, and board members. The mood eventually turned in Murdoch's favor. Time will tell, however, how well his leadership will play out and how the public will receive the *Journal* in the future. His creative genius reflects his willingness to take risks and points to his leadership style among associates within his expanding organization. If organizational wisdom calls for creativity and character in order to succeed, leaders will need to bear these important factors in mind as they further their ambitions and strategic plans.

Creativity is often not welcomed in organizations clinging to the status quo. This resistance factor is often found, for example, among employees, supporters, and volunteers serving nonprofits such as charitable, religious, medical, educational, philanthropic, and social-service institutions. We simply reach a comfortable niche that justifies the status quo, and we expect the sources of revenue to continue indefinitely. But a financial crisis serves as a shocking wake-up call to a new phase of reality. This no doubt was happening in the Dow Jones Co. when confronted with the Murdoch buy offer.

The spirit of creativity required at such moments actually offers the opportunity to view the crisis as an unexpected "friend" rather than the "enemy." A change of attitude is awkward but necessary if creativity is to have a chance to operate, lifting everyone to a fresh level of engagement. The anxiety of the Bancroft family could have been less painful if they had faced these changing realities earlier. Whatever the shortcomings for owners or management, the need to acknowledge the necessity for change is inescapable for organizations in need of improvement. Neither followers nor leaders can neglect nurturing a creative spirit when confronting the long-term welfare of their organization. Creativity is essential when coupled with wise risk taking and should be constantly encouraged in every organization.

SEE SOLUTIONS WHEN OTHERS SEE BARRIERS

Much of our creativity ought to be directed toward problem solving rather than denial or escape. At a Tallberg Forum in Sweden in which I participated, representatives and leaders from over seventy countries studied the theme "How in the World Can We Live Together?" The focus was on the nearly three billion impoverished people of the world who exist on less than $2 per day. In parts of Africa, 70 percent of the population earns even less. While the wealthier nations do supply large amounts of relief, especially when starvation strikes, such charitable efforts do not facilitate realistic development. There is a well-known Chinese proverb that makes the distinction between development and charity clear: "Give hungry persons fish, and they will be hungry tomorrow. Teach persons how to fish, and they will never be hungry again." Another essential task of wealthy nations is to teach the importance of sharing their increased supply of fish and thereby avoid a glut in one community at the expense of others. The obligation of responsible organizations around the world is not difficult to imagine when we are faced with the global crisis of hunger.

Sadly, we are divided by many intractable conflicts, including terrorism. Among the global issues calling for attention are the supply and cost of oil, climate change, human rights, HIV/AIDS and other pandemic diseases, and the depletion of natural resources—especially pure water, which the Tallberg gathering indicated will be a greater problem than the oil concerns of today. Think about it. If we are truly to be global leaders of tomorrow, how much creative cooperation can we expect among ourselves to address these challenges? Or should we simply anticipate a growing loss of human lives? Can we build a satisfactory framework for a sustainable future as we work toward an expanding network of global interdependence? Can we confront conflicts and debates with greater imagination and enthusiasm to enhance the quality of life within our global society? Thank God for the Bill and Melinda Gates and Warren Buffetts of the world, but their tribe of donors is insufficient. Is the human apocalypse of despair an unavoidable possibility that awaits us?

My own approach to organizational problems is to harness our limited energies and resources into a spiritual framework that releases the needed creativity and goodwill that lie within us. Many of us are unwilling to take any risk that exposes this spiritual dimension of reality. We need to come clean with ourselves and express without apology our inner drive for divine dependence. Unfortunately, we are often guided instead by stubborn doubts and pride that prevent us from being drawn into the empowering circle of spiritual realities. Wise leaders with enduring legacies have learned these lessons and have been inspired by their own faith, hope, and love to build a common bond of trust within their institutions, companies, or nations. To reach this end, followers and leaders need to bear in mind the following basic guidelines:[3]

1. Love life to the fullest. To love less is to shortchange ourselves before God. The purpose of our lives is to live in a manner that honors the unseen divine image within each person.
2. Know that the risks we take in life are not of equal value. Discern priorities through honest prayer (ranking them if you will) that instill a sense of divine dependence. Such an attitude prepares us for life's inescapable trade-offs and separates what is acceptable before God from what isn't. We then discover what we have forgotten, namely, that the ends do not justify the means.
3. Outline a hierarchy of values based on integrity, respect, and the dignity of human life that will guide you in determining what is negotiable or nonnegotiable in human society, where dehumanizing trade-offs occur repeatedly. When we value life cheaply, we neither honor ourselves nor the Creator whose image we reflect.
4. Nurture creative spirit through scriptural reading, disciplined study, and meaningful discussions. Prayer is the channel for asking God to direct one's path with humility. Be open to the possibilities of change that can improve organizations and relationships.
5. Listen to trusting voices that challenge your thoughts and assumptions while also giving you encouragement to pursue ideas that truly advance human life. The power of good ideas is greater than we think.
6. Place ultimate trust in God over yourself and others. Be led by God's Spirit, not your feelings or the voices of those who are always asking you and me to "play it safe."
7. Practice a life of thanksgiving and praise for the divine gifts and talents you and I enjoy and often take for granted until they are

abused. Increasing the spirit of thanksgiving enables us to share more willingly with others.

8. Discover God's amazing creation daily; let your actions reflect and uphold the resources of the environment, created for us to enjoy and share with one another. Don't be selfish or wasteful of God's gifts.

9. Seek and pray daily for courage to make a positive difference in life and, by divine grace, to be a blessing not only to family and friends but also to strangers and even enemies. When we stop caring for our enemies, we actually stop caring for ourselves to do the right thing.

10. Educate yourself to be well informed not only on the trends of the times but on the character of those asking for your support and loyalty and wanting you to follow their leadership. In other words, understand the zeitgeist (or contextual intelligence and prevailing ethics) of each age, past and present.[4] Ask yourself, "To what extent should the lessons of the past inform and guide me in my present context?"

11. Seek to cultivate a deepening friendship with the Source of Life and foster others' participation in this process. The Russian theologian Alexander Schmemann reminds us in his ecumenical spirit that "the world is a perpetual revelation of God about himself to humanity; it is only a means of communion; of this constant, free, and joyful encounter—with the only context of life—with the life of life itself—with God."[5]

While the preceding points are all connected and overlap, I find it helps to review them separately and regularly to prepare for the expected and unexpected challenges of each day. From this framework and spirit, I find myself able to anticipate possibilities where others see only barriers and lack of hope. In particular, intimacy with the Source of Life deepens our understanding of trust, hope, faithfulness, and integrity as we face the divine mysteries and unanswered questions we encounter. At the heart of one's everyday prayer life is the simple asking for divine grace and mercy to uphold us—the gifts we enjoy will exceed what we deserve, reminding us that we live each day from grace to grace and from mercy to mercy with every breath we take. We have no other guarantees in life. Herein is the core rationale for practicing an attitude of humility.

CULTIVATE DISCERNMENT IN EVALUATING IDEAS

When we are considering ideas that might become "solutions" to issues confronting our organizations, we require a deep discernment to evaluate which of the probable "answers" to our problems we should adopt. First, the exercise of "contextual intelligence" is an approach that might prove helpful in addressing issues such as government intervention, global unrest, demographics, social mores, technology, and employee concerns. As we pull together useful information regarding a strategic and creative response to any specific problem, we are able to move forward. Our approaches and ideas need to be viewed from the perspective of the prevailing context under question, which in turn allows us to employ contrasting styles and input among followers and leaders within the organization. Many styles of leadership are required in changing times, calling for a flexible menu of "right ideas" led by the "right people."

To cultivate discernment in evaluating ideas calls for a balcony overview that enables us to raise additional questions based on our analysis of comparable situations:[6]

—What's causing the present distress for our organization?
—What internal contradictions does the present issue raise for us? And what histories do we have from the past?
—To what extent will the expression of our ideas compound the issues before us, thereby heightening the conflict?
—To what extent does the idea simply reflect the dynamics of our problems without providing answers?
—If we pursue the idea before us, will we reach a breaking point?
—Will the ideas being considered restore our equilibrium?
—Are we aware of the avoidance patterns of this community, and will the impact of the idea under consideration be a plus or a minus?
—Will the current leadership and the idea fit?
—Is our issue sufficiently ripe, or is the community ready enough for our idea?
—Will this primary idea bring forth the change we desire?
—What losses can we envision if we pursue the idea under consideration? Are we ready to live with these trade-offs?
—Is the leader's role enhanced through this idea?
—If we follow the idea under consideration, will we reduce our conflict?

In short, we must be doubly aware that there are no easy answers when leading an organization. Leaders and followers must always remind themselves of this reality. Next, we must create a brief sanctuary of quiet for ourselves (and others) before sharing our final response; such reflection is wise prior to agreeing to any decision or idea that might later prove to be either useful or harmful to the organization. Bear in mind that wisdom is having the "right insight" before exercising the decision. The risk factor can be minimized but not eliminated; our discernments are never complete, but we nevertheless need to make every effort to evaluate all ideas being presented. My own experience has been that all of us make mistakes. This is why leadership normally calls for a shared relationship with followers to help discern what's desired and which combination of team building is best for the organization's future.

It was my practice as the chief executive of a graduate theological school to say to faculty and staff that none of us has a monopoly on suggestions. For the enhancement of the school, each of us had an obligation to critique one another. My own ideas were no exception to this general guideline as we moved ahead; the seminary's progress was always a team effort. To further reinforce this joint campus spirit, on the eve of my retirement from the seminary after a long presidency and professorship, our family established an endowment fund to provide an annual award for an outstanding member of the seminary community in recognition and appreciation for his or her creative ideas and services in advancing the quality of our life together. The annual person awarded is elected by the seminary's board of directors based on nominations from faculty, administrative staff, and students. The final candidate receives the Community Service Award and is recognized at the annual commencement celebration.

Frankly, ideas from the CEO of any organization, I believe, should be viewed as a "jump start" to get the entire community to think more imaginatively and to sense their own responsibility for the organization's improvement and fulfillment of its mission. An important task of responsible leadership is to model and encourage a creative spirit in which there is freedom to exchange ideas and welcome suggestions that will be heard and considered.

Too many organizations, as reported by Gary Neilson, Bruce Pasternack, and Karen Van Nuys of the Booz Allen Hamilton consulting firm, have a passive-aggressive attitude within the workplace that undermines creative productivity and is unhealthy. The passive-aggressive organizational style indicates that the levels of management may react with a smile and a nod, just enough to get by.[7]

Having tight control in an organization is a self-defeating goal. In contrast, healthier organizations are flexible and adaptable to change. This looser style of responsible leadership in organizations contributes to resilience and ought to be found more often.[8] While the consultants from Booz Allen Hamilton focused on project-oriented business organizations, I suspect that the above descriptions of flexible control could be applied to nonprofit institutions as well. Nonprofits can also have a tendency toward passive-aggressive behavior, sometimes hidden behind platitudes and piety. Long-established organizations are often less resilient to change and tend to focus on past achievements of their founders, who actually may have had a greater commitment to reform than their successors do.

Whether the organization is profit or nonprofit, the passive-aggressive ethic hurts those with a creative initiative who want to proceed more quickly without being accused of second-guessing leaders to a less satisfying feeling of fulfilling their responsibilities.[9] When the healthy impulses of subordinates and followers to share ideas are not encouraged, a slowdown in creative conduct gradually ensues. Is it any wonder, then, why action of any kind becomes scarce? This causes erstwhile doers to look elsewhere to invest themselves where taking a risk is more promising. The absence of imaginative confrontation in such organizations is a disguise for intransigence. Unhealthy organizations suffer from an imbalance of either too much control at the top or seemingly no control at all. It seems difficult to maintain the proper tension that nurtures creativity and initiative.

In any context of change, it is to the organization's advantage to be flexible rather than entrenched, and to be adaptable and thereby avoid chronic fatigue. The passive-aggressive organization needs to clarify the scope of its authority to align properly its incentives and goals and to avoid wasteful games, such as pursuing agreements through backroom politics. Transforming passive-aggressive organizations into healthy and resilient organizations calls for honesty within a problem-solving climate that has visionary personnel who welcome change. Together, all interested parties can work for positive results, encouraged by a cooperative spirit of discernment in pursuing new ideas.

This pursuit of new ideas goes through a rapid process when the leader is also blessed with an abundant spirit of creativity. This is evident at Costco, a large retail merchandising company. According to

Fortune magazine, when Jim Sinegal, cofounder and longtime CEO of Costco, visits one of the company's large warehouse stores, the excitement among the employees rises.[10] They know their leader has ideas and expects ideas from them as well. Sinegal is not a spectator boss; he is creativity personified, in action that generates excitement and, I suspect, anxiety as well. Sinegal is seen as the creative "connoisseur of detail" with a no-nonsense attitude toward the status quo. Sinegal believes in change when needed. His aim is simple; he wishes to be the most creative center of business in his type of work, and he supports the needs of shoppers as well as suggestions and ideas from his people.

Apparently, Costco is doing a good job, with over $59 billion in sales from 488 warehouse locations in 2008. The company stood at number twenty-eight in the Fortune 500 and is the fourth largest retailer in the country, even though Costco has eighty-two fewer warehouses than its nearest rival, Sam's Club. Costco nevertheless generates about $20 billion more in sales, motivated by Sinegal's spirit of creativity. Yet he's modestly compensated. Sinegal earned $450,000 in salary and bonus in 2007, which isn't high by CEO standards today. (We will discuss leadership compensation in a later chapter.)

And yet the reality in your neighborhood may be that the Costco style of organizational creativity is alien and unwanted. Understanding this process of creativity is a complex discernment of ideas related to every context; realities, trade-offs, and threats may be involved. What to accept and whom to follow will always be issues for discussion and discernment.

PURSUE VISIONARY LEADERS AND FOLLOWERS: REWARDS FAR OUTWEIGH RISKS

In the final analysis, visionary leaders and followers hold the keys that unlock the doors to creativity, leading often to good fortune that far outweighs the limits imposed by the status quo. Creative leadership matters. Followership that is willing to learn also matters. Leaders and followers who excel are aware that no single person has a monopoly on ideas. Those who are wise listen to all suggestions and are constantly open to shared leadership. Visionary leaders know from experience that one of the

> deepest of truths about the cry of the human heart is that it is so often muted, so often a cry that is never uttered. To be sure there

are needs and feelings that we express quite openly. Lying deeper are emotions we share only with loved ones and deeper still the things we tell no one. We die with much unsaid.[11]

This observation was made by John W. Gardner, founder of Common Cause, whose distinguished life of service intersected with persons of many backgrounds and outlooks.

All leaders worth following have a wide range of lifestyles—some more to our liking than others. Among twentieth-century political heads of state were those who attended the Yalta Summit associated with World War II—Winston Churchill, Franklin D. Roosevelt, and Josef Stalin. On the other hand, a lower profile of leadership and its influence was seen in Albert Einstein. Howard Gardner of Harvard University, however, has focused on yet another group of visionary and unexpected leaders in his book *Leading Minds: An Anatomy of Leadership*.[12] His selection highlights the following persons: Margaret Mead, J. Robert Oppenheimer, Robert Maynard Hutchins, Alfred P. Sloan Jr., George C. Marshall, Pope John XXIII, Eleanor Roosevelt, Martin Luther King Jr., Margaret Thatcher, Jean Monnet, and Mahatma Gandhi.

Who would be on your list? Whom would you single out as a model to emulate? These questions could lead to a lively discussion with your colleagues, family, friends, or study group about the most viable models of visionary leadership that are worth pursuing. Also, we could question their styles of leading and ask how interconnected their roles of followership and leadership were. How would they compare with your leadership judgments and practices? Among your choices, do you think the individuals you picked saw themselves as unexpected leaders who surprised themselves by the final outcomes in their lives?

Another interesting list of ten visionary leaders published in *Fortune* magazine by Jim Collins in 2003 included the following:[13]

1. Charles Coffin, whose lack of fame is a mark of his greatness, invented the General Electric Co. Coffin created a system of genius that did not depend on him, namely, the first research laboratory and the idea of systematic management development. Jack Welch, GE's well-known CEO, vastly improved GE's management system but did not invent the concept; instead, he enhanced it. Coffin built the stage on which other CEOs like Jack Welch could make contributions.

2. Bill Allen, following World War II, took the Boeing Co., known for its bombers, and transformed it by producing new commercial jets—707, 727, 737, and 747. He aimed higher than what most of the airline industry thought possible.

3. Sam Walton reached beyond his promotional charisma to establish Walmart as the world's largest retailer, able to provide better things affordably for persons of lesser means.

4. George Merck II gave to his industry a vision of providing affordable medicines for people everywhere.

5. Darwin Smith did more than save the company when he transformed Kimberly-Clark in 1971 from a paper-mill company into the leading paper-based consumer products company.

6. James Burke, the former CEO of Johnson & Johnson, did much more than pull Tylenol capsules off the shelves in response to the cyanide poisoning crisis in 1982; he lifted the Johnson & Johnson credo to a higher ethical standard of commitment and practice as a living document that pointed the company ahead of such crises.

7. David Maxwell in 1981 transformed a mortgage lender company, Fannie Mae, and saved it from disaster, setting an example of democratizing home ownership and helping to make the American dream possible for millions of new homeowners.

8. William McKnight in 1929 displayed creativity through the 3M Corp., allowing his people to pursue fledgling new ideas with freedom to grow and create many helpful new products, like the Post-It.

9. Katherine Graham, the young widow who decided on August 3, 1963, not to give up, took over ownership of the *Washington Post* and widened its impact from a local to a national paper. She risked it all when her newspaper published the Pentagon Papers, which revealed government deception concerning the Vietnam War. For the *Washington Post* to publish the materials, she faced government prosecution under the Espionage Act and endangered her ownership of the paper as well as employment for her people. Nevertheless, she stood up for the press's freedom despite threats from the Nixon White House.

10. David Packard, cofounder of Hewlett-Packard, established not only a unique product but, equally as important, a style of leadership that turned the company into a club where everyone's dignity and respect were acknowledged at work. He shared an

open-door workspace among his fellow engineers and identi-
fied with them as colleagues. He indeed played an instrumental
role in transforming followers into leaders and leaders into
listeners. He felt strongly that those who were in partnership
with him had a moral right to share in the wealth created by
the company.

For Jim Collins, author of *Good to Great*, these ordinary/
extraordinary leaders continue as examples for us to emulate, serving as
creative leaders for the organizations they served. Through their efforts,
the gifts of creativity, vision, and tenacity benefited their organizations.
As Collins points out, "It was their deep sense of connectedness to
the organizations they ran. . . . They understood the central paradox
of exceptional corporate leadership. On the one hand, a company
depends more on the CEO than any other individual. Only the CEO
can make the really big decisions."[14] But on the other hand, the CEO
knows that he or she can succeed only when working together with
colleagues as a team.

In highlighting the important role of creative leadership that matters, we also need to acknowledge that these leaders represent less than
10 percent of the total puzzle. Ninety percent also depend on those
surrounding them. This observation does not diminish the leader's
catalytic input that ignites the 90 percent eager to pursue the signal
to move forward. Of course, the formula also depends on the leader's
competence to act, the subject of our next chapter.

2

Competence

Have you heard of Wendy Kopp? She is a remarkable leader in spite of her shyness, with a burning passion to raise a new generation of competent leadership in America that would inspire young people from all social classes to make a difference with their lives. She is seeking to demonstrate that achieving competence in leadership matters, enabling young people to participate in transforming society and its organizations to higher levels of achievement. Her message is directed broadly to college students, recent graduates, and high school students.

Her organization, Teach for America (TFA), recruits the finest graduates from our colleges and universities to teach for two years in troubled high schools. Recent graduates accepted in the programs are first put through a vigorous summer training program. The recruits often set aside their undergraduate majors and postpone their career paths until after their social service experiences through TFA. In 2006, TFA attracted 19,000 applicants and accepted 2,400. It is reported that "Kopp's nonprofit is one of the largest hirers of college seniors according to CollegeGrad.com—bigger than Microsoft, Procter & Gamble or General Electric."[1] This is certainly larger than any entering class of professional graduate schools in whatever field of endeavor.

Wendy's dream took shape almost twenty years ago in her last year as an undergraduate student at Princeton University. It was expressed in her senior thesis, titled "A Plan and Argument for the Creation of a National Teachers Corps," and is known today as TFA. Her ambition for the idea and her zeal were expressed in a letter to President George H. W. Bush, encouraging him to start a two-year service program similar in spirit to the Peace Corps. In response, she received an employment rejection letter. I suspect no one read her letter carefully. She was also rejected by a number of corporations until she decided to launch the teaching corps herself.

She didn't let rejection stop her. She believed in the intrinsic worth of her idea and the need for educated competence in leadership. So she began making a series of cold calls to CEOs and foundation executives. Eventually, Rex Adams, a leader at Mobil, agreed to give her a modest grant of $26,000, and Dick Fisher, then CEO of Morgan Stanley, donated office space for her use. A small skeleton crew for TFA began to recruit top graduates from colleges and universities to teach in poor urban areas. It wasn't long before other corporate funders caught the spark of Wendy's enthusiasm to engage bright graduates in reaching young people with hidden talents in our public schools. Everyone contacted, it seems, including high school students, shared her wish to raise the standards for competence while building a caring spirit among future leaders.

Since the inception of TFA, many of its alums have found meaningful employment in leading companies in this country, as well as acceptance in a wide range of professional schools. These students have an expanded spirit to do good for others over self. They are driven by a higher calling of self-fulfillment, and some, no doubt, will become tomorrow's social entrepreneurs. Most organizations that possess an enterprising spirit—profit and nonprofit—are seeking competent and talented leaders who are willing to take risks and exercise their imagination as Wendy did. For instance, Pittsburgh Theological Seminary in 1997 began a Summer Youth Institute to identify future clergy and lay leaders for the churches and its institutions among rising high school seniors. The students attend a two-week program taught by the seminary's faculty, drawing young people from over forty states and territories to date. Future programs for high school young people, college students, and seminarians might consider new ventures in social entrepreneurship that address financial realities in communities and religious institutions and find ways to assist them in improving their economic conditions, thus enabling them to reduce their dependence on welfare and other funding sources.

Leadership that matters in today's global society focuses on common needs that acknowledge and support our diversity. We can no longer afford to be parochial religiously, socially, or economically; the unfortunate thing is that in spite of our travels around the world, we are actually missing the grassroots conversations that count and, accept it or not, are not spoken in English. Those of us who are limited to English might be overlooking in our travels the informative factors that could make a real difference if heard in the languages of today's global village. Cultural misunderstandings hinder our empathy and effectiveness in decision making and also in building healthy relationships with one another. In directing any organization, one is wise to make an earnest effort to overcome the cultural barriers that still exist. Humility and hindsight become useful guides to enable us to adapt in every situation. Most of us still lack the intercultural knowledge to connect effectively on many levels with one another. With time, however, we can begin to understand the importance of flexibility in reaching goals as we learn the art of risk taking between the yin and yang found in our lives.

Recruiting promising college and university graduates to a worthy cause is at the core of TFA success. Not everyone who wishes to serve under TFA sponsorship is selected, however—only those who have caught the vision and importance of educating students to become competent leaders and qualified mentors. TFA hoped to have eight thousand teachers in the field before the end of 2009. This ambitious goal helps us understand why the board of trustees of TFA is so excited about Wendy and her team. Wendy's mission is a breath of fresh air and hope for tomorrow's organizations seeking competent and caring leaders. As CEO Ken Thompson of Wachovia comments, "I'm bowled over by Wendy's absolute belief that TFA can change the world."[2] How many profit and nonprofit organizations are there today that would like to have Wendy's zeal for competence in their organization? Teachers' unions and governmental standards locally and nationally should also be engaged with TFA to advance public education and future policy direction in raising standards for youth.

Competence is indeed an essential factor behind winning organizations. None of us are exempt from expecting the highest standards of performance from ourselves and our organizations. Any organization undergoing transformation has the wish to transcend its past on all levels. Essential to the process is for each of us, whatever our role, to overcome that "nobody feeling" holding us back while undermining our confidence. To build a quality team we need to focus in every case on doing the right thing whatever the nature of our organizational service. Improving our competence and confidence will lift our spirits, transform attitudes, and foster a greater willingness to take risks beyond what we thought was possible.

Each of us, I believe, can make meaningful contributions in a world of challenging changes and unsafe circumstances. We can also promote peace and freedom without being mesmerized by the constant anxiety fostered by television and the news media. Every conflict or tragedy adds to our distrust of one another. It seems none of us really feels safe today. Military and nuclear forces in themselves cannot bring enduring victory to the "winning" side. As we listen with greater awareness to one another's needs and hopes in this technologically charged world, we begin to realize that national boundaries are becoming an illusion of protection. We need, instead, to infuse our creative imagination with a range of core competencies that provide a positive sense of togetherness for the twenty-first century. This is the hope of Bill Gates of Microsoft, who is sufficiently confident already to be creating his company's next home of the future. I imagine Microsoft employees are not alone in asking themselves, "To what extent should we allow ourselves to be influenced by yesterday's and today's violence? Or are we simply captive to past and present suspicions that prevent us from working for a more humane life within our global village? Are we content with the present status quo and its debilitating nature to rule our tomorrows?"

Who among us truly wishes to be overcome by yesterday's unwise decisions and today's destructive conflicts? While doing research for this book, I was invited to spend a spring term as a visiting academic fellow at Oxford University, hosted by Harris Manchester College. I recall reading one morning in the faculty senior common room, a London newspaper called *The Independent*. The April 16, 2006, headline read, "America Meets the New Superpower," and the accompanying photo showed the red flag of the People's Republic of China eclipsing the stars and stripes of the United States. The news story suggested that America is in a state of "managed decline" as a superpower and that China is moving rapidly to overtake the United States within twenty-five years. China is now regarded as the fourth economic superpower in the world behind the United States, Japan, and Russia.

The article noted that China's president Hu Jintao was first paying a visit in Seattle to Bill Gates of Microsoft and CEO Howard Schultz of Starbucks before seeing President George W. Bush in Washington DC. Gates and Schultz are both enterprising and visionary business leaders well aware that the rank of any organization or country is never permanent in a shifting global society. Today's challenging international framework confronts global leadership everywhere; no one can stay safe on the sidelines, avoiding twenty-first-century realities. Our global and national interests are interrelated today more than ever, and profit and nonprofit organizations everywhere need to acknowledge this beyond their local interests. If we resist widening our horizons, we will be unable to apply new solutions to overcome our long history of repeatable conflicts.

OVERCOME SELF-DOUBT: YOU'RE MUCH BETTER THAN YOU THINK YOU ARE

Eurocentric countries, including all of us in North America, increasingly doubt their capacity to compete successfully in the future. Our fears and tensions have been heightened in recent years through political skirmishes and international struggles with terrorists at home and abroad, and nuclear dangers are proliferating in an anxious world. We worry about the nature of our destiny; we may no longer be able to protect our existing territories and advantages. How do we overcome the growing threat posed by the inevitable forces of change? How do we manage decline as a superpower? Are we following the path of the United Kingdom since World War II? Should we cheer ourselves up, claiming that we are much better than we think we are becoming? Have we lost ourselves in empty rhetoric? Unless we are realistic with ourselves, we will continue to drift into a downward orbit, trying to hold on to the status quo while suspecting that the changing realities are more than we can bear.

Scriptural reality has taught us to uphold "faith, hope, and love," knowing that the greatest of these is still love (1 Cor. 13:13). In our experiences, however, we know that this isn't how it often turns out in life. We might pledge allegiance to the motto that appears on our dollar bills, "In God We Trust," but it seems we have less confidence in God when the dollar's value sinks, reminding us again that the financial status quo is always an up-and-down affair. Is this why we resist change? Are our religious traditions too oriented to the status quo? Are our faith teachings no longer subject to the changing winds of the Spirit? Presbyterians refer to their historic church heritage as being "reformed and always reforming," acknowledging the onward leading of God's Spirit in their lives. And yet as a Presbyterian I wonder if we at times work diligently to subvert the reforming side of the church's tradition.

Perhaps we are honestly unwilling to accept diversity and change at home and abroad in our interpretations of sacred Scripture.

The fears we harbor today are nurtured in part by our many faith claims. As we listen to voices in our world, people everywhere appear threatened by change. Today's followers and leaders need to engage their public with candor and a clear assessment of their situation. How honest can we be with ourselves? When was the last time each of us took a "Know yourself" survey? How can we know our collective capabilities without knowing better our personal selves? Now is the time not only for religious institutions but also for businesses and governments to submit themselves to thorough self-assessment.

Professor Peter Drucker, a prolific management thinker, published an article in the *Harvard Business Review* titled "Managing Oneself," inviting us to initiate a self-assessment around key questions.[3] Begin, he said, with one question: "What are my strengths?" We may know less about our strengths and weaknesses than we have been willing to admit. We need a feedback analysis to help us listen to others as well as to our inner selves. So try this: After deciding on an important matter, write down what you think will happen and then review your journal nine to twelve months later to compare the results with your forecast. The outcome may surprise you, but it will also inform you of your decision-making skills along with those of fellow colleagues who participated in the process with you.

Drucker claims that this feedback process was practiced by John Calvin and Ignatius of Loyola. While neither of them was perfect, both had a significant effect on Protestants and Catholics in their respective traditions. The whole point of this exercise is to illustrate the importance of concentrating on your strengths. First, as Drucker emphasizes, we need to place ourselves where our strengths can show results.

Second, improve your strengths; otherwise they will become weaknesses with time. We not only need to stay in physical shape; we also need to stay in mental shape. We need to continually improve our present skills and knowledge base. This is what education is all about—enhancing strengths and curbing weaknesses.

Third, are you being controlled by your intellectual hubris and thus contributing to a disruptive outlook? This may have been the case among the critics of Galileo. Without enhancing our skills and knowledge, we cannot advance our strengths. Instead, we increase our arrogance and anger, we stifle our ability to learn, and we show insensitivity and rudeness in how we relate to others. How often have our personal manners based on our hubris created battle lines inhibiting future connections?

The next key question to ask yourself is "How do I perform?" Given your strengths, how do you get things done? The healthy maintenance of our strengths influences the quality of our performance, which depends on how we view ourselves. For instance, are we primarily readers or listeners? President Dwight Eisenhower was more a reader than a listener, and this influenced how he interacted with reporters at press conferences. Presidents Franklin D. Roosevelt and Harry Truman saw themselves primarily as listeners. So was Lyndon Johnson, but he didn't know he was a listener, which actually worked against him in his presidency. John Kennedy was a reader and made good use of that fact as he assembled a brilliant group of writers on his staff.

How we perform is influenced in part by how we learn—from reading, listening, writing, or questioning. There is no single right way to learn. But good listening is an immense aid to effective leaders. In our formal educational process we tend not to recognize this reality sufficiently. Drucker is asking us is to reflect on the real possibility that we are unlikely to change ourselves, given our preference to curtail our learning and listening. For instance, I am left-handed, and I broke my left arm when I was three years old. My parents worked diligently to influence me at that time to become right-handed during my healing process. After the healing, I reverted to my left hand. Nonetheless, whatever our preferences, we still need to improve our style in order to make effective contact in our presentations and to become more competent. Drucker maintains that far more energy is needed to move from incompetence to mediocrity than to move from first-rate performance to excellence.[4] Understanding who we are helps us to overcome self-doubt and improve on the talents we have.

RECOGNIZE AND USE YOUR NATURAL GIFTS

What (or who) do you want to be? That's a familiar question often heard in conversations with children and young adults and among peer groups of all ages. Many answering the question are quite sure of themselves. Others, however, wrestle with choices as they oscillate before various appealing visions or find themselves influenced by a range of mentors. As my wife, Doris, and I learned in raising our three children, there is little correlation, it seems, between one's college major and later vocational choice. It appears that the more talents we possess, the longer it takes to make a choice that will recognize and use our natural gifts. This should remind us not to be overly concerned, as some parents are, in urging a particular path or direction for children too early. Hopefully, the advice we share as mentors ought to encourage young people not to be limited to the subjects they study. A narrow focus too early in life can curtail a necessary self-exploration.

In my own case, I showed interest in many subject areas thanks to my early readings (I'm grateful to the school librarians in my youth), writing exercises, and listening and speaking to a host of individuals, including strangers I met who told me their stories. Subjects that held particular interest in my first year of college were economics, history, law, and psychology. In my second college year, I had temporary employment delivering Christmas mail and then later had a weekend job selling shoes. Like my classmates, I asked, "What do I want to do during the best part of each day for the rest of my life? What is it that I really enjoy? What would be the most challenging task for me?" Delivering mail and selling shoes were good exercises in helping me to reflect as I searched my feelings and prayerfully reflected for a sense of direction.

I enjoyed studying and reading. I also liked people and found it interesting to explore with them the questions they were raising for their own lives. During one college summer, I had a position working in a government employment office interviewing persons who were receiving their unemployment checks. This also proved to be a learning experience. I discovered that I appreciated having variety in my life that widened my horizon from studies to sports, summer youth camps to travel adventures and work experiences. I then asked myself how I could find time to study, meet interesting people, and engage in a variety of experiences all within a single vocational field. In time, the pastoral ministry seemed to be my calling. At first I followed it tentatively, but after graduation from Occidental College and a year of seminary, I felt I had found a "real fit" and viewed my choice as a "divine call" for me. Later, church officers in our Presbyterian system of governance agreed. I also saw my call as a two-way journey—you can be called into one vocation as well as being called from it to pursue another field as God leads in your life. The overall aim is always to show an openness to God's calling throughout one's lifetime. This has been an important guideline for me, for to feel imprisoned in one's vocation is deadly.

Faithfulness before God ought to be our primary concern, which may include a wide range of calls that bring fulfillment throughout one's lifetime. In my case, my first few years were in parish ministry; after I completed my doctorate in theology, my ministry became centered in graduate theological education, where I discovered my talent being used to its utmost. Through my years of service in higher education (seminary, college, and university), I have felt fulfilled. My wife and I thank God for the direction of our shared life and for our children and their families.

My life has been governed by a sense of divine call, which I believe everyone can experience, but it is difficult to explain. It would be easier if we could take a long walk and discuss it together. The bottom line is that we are all called to do our utmost in service to others, who, like ourselves, share the divine image. This service can take many shapes and vocations. There is no hierarchy in my understanding of a "call." It is simply humankind at its best, fulfilling our stewardship of the gift of life and the created environment, honoring the divine trust placed in us. This sense of "call" should never be thought of as an opportunity for special privilege belonging to any class of people, whatever their status might be. A sense of call can belong to all God's people in every age. We are all sojourners ("nobodies" if you wish), who believe by divine grace that we are also "somebodies" who are recognized in our service to one another as followers and leaders, depending on the tasks and circumstances life brings us.

For me, this call is an expanding vision of service to others. For instance, one summer I was invited to be a visiting scholar at the Graduate School of Business at Stanford University, where I had the good fortune to become acquainted with John W. Gardner, a distinguished teacher, scholar, public servant, and leader. He was a senior distinguished faculty member at Stanford and known to millions of citizens in his later life as the founder of Common Cause. He wisely observed in his writings the following for our reflection:

> Leaders must understand that for most men and women the driving energies are latent. Some individuals are unaware of their potentialities, some are sleep walking through the routines of life and some are succumbed to a sense of defeat. What leaders see on the surface can be discouraging—people, even very able people, caught in the routines of life, thinking short term, plowing narrow self-beneficial furrows through life. What leaders have to remember is that somewhere under that somnolent surface is the creature that builds civilizations, the dreamer of dreams, and the risk taker. And, remember that the leader must reach down to the springs that never dry up, the ever-fresh springs of the human spirit.[5]

BE A LIFELONG STUDENT—
PRACTICE! PRACTICE! PRACTICE!

When I completed Virgil Junior High School in Los Angeles, I quit the violin even though I had been a part of our school's award-winning Little Symphony. There were one hundred of us playing under a tough, disciplined taskmaster, Conductor Vernon Leidig. He was committed to us and to classical music. We literally felt like "nobodies," and he was dedicated to transforming us collectively into "somebodies" through our early-morning and after-school rehearsals that exceeded the credits we received for the music course. Ours was a three-year middle school (seventh, eighth, and ninth grades). Those of us in the orchestra felt we worked harder than all the sports teams put together. After becoming the chair of the second-violin section and anticipating going to high school soon, I knew that classical music would always have a fond place in my heart, but I felt that I didn't have the talent to become a symphony player. It wasn't my gift or my dream. I knew I would have a difficult time, however, convincing my mother that continuing violin lessons would be a waste of her limited funds; she was a widow and a working mother raising two children. "And besides, Mom," I said, "I want to learn to play baseball in high school." She reluctantly went along with my wishes.

At Dorsey High School in Los Angeles, I signed up for tenth-grade baseball. The coach said to me, "I see by your name 'Calian' [the 'ian' was his clue] that you must be of Armenian descent. The American Armenians I have had on past baseball teams have all been good ballplayers, so I'll sign you up without a trial." I knew that was a mistake, given my inexperience. After all, I had been spending my time practicing the violin. This was going to be my first serious effort at baseball, the all-American sport my older cousin, Harry Maghakian, favored when he gave me his used first-base glove because I was a left-hander like he was.

It didn't take the coach long to learn that this American Armenian was a real novice at baseball. My offense was hitting the coach in a workout with one of my throws from first base to home plate. The coach had one rule for all the players—every mistake on the field would cost you a lap around the track. I was spending more time running around the track than playing baseball. At the end of the season, I knew there would be no more baseball for me. Besides, I was sure I wouldn't make the coach's list. Instead, my unofficial jogging career had begun, which I still maintain to this day. The experience did teach me a lesson, however. The secret to excellence, whether in sports or music, is practice, practice, and more practice. This fact is especially true if you are lacking in talent. Also, not to overlook Drucker's point, I discovered that neither baseball nor the violin would be part of my strengths and would never bring me to the threshold of excellence even if I died trying. I wasn't downcast, however, because I knew I had other talents and that God had an unfolding purpose for my life, as is the case for each of us until we finally retire at death (Ps. 138:8).

From my professional teaching experience later in life, I discovered that "practice" was simply a code term for disciplined study on a lifetime basis. Believe it or not, we are called to be lifelong students in whatever we do that is worthy of our time and efforts. This is certainly true for effective pastoral ministry, which can be said to be my vocational profession as well as my calling. Hopefully, others can say the same about their vocational task, whatever it might be. We may shift in our vocational calling from one endeavor to another during the course of our lives, but the call to practice and study always remains in whatever task engages us the best part of each day. If we are feeling fatigued in our work, perhaps we may need a vacation or even a change to a new calling altogether. Whatever the case, we must be honest with ourselves and others; otherwise we are living a wasted life that is unfulfilling and unfaithful to those we serve. We need to engage in frank dialogue in these matters with colleagues we trust.

The very nature of competence requires adequate time for study, practice, and rest. This is as true for every member of a parish, including the pastor and staff, as it is for a medical community of health providers or any other vocational commitment. Perhaps you have read about the surgical teams who have accidentally left clamps, sponges, and other items inside patients. Maybe the mistakes were the result of job fatigue or neglect. The *New England Journal of Medicine* reported that 1,500 patients nationwide experience such errors each year, according to a study by researchers at Brigham and Women's Hospital and Harvard School of Public Health. A total of three million dollars was paid out in the Massachusetts cases in legal settlements. In many cases the embedded objects required additional surgery, and one patient died of complications. Of course, 1,500 patients among roughly 28 million surgeries that year in the United States is a small number. I suspect, however, that none of us wants to be among the 1,500. No one on a medical team would consider that acceptable, said Dr. Donald Berwick, president of the nonprofit Institute for Healthcare Improvement.[6]

Malpractice in any field raises insurance costs, but, more important, it causes a loss of trust. I suspect no profession, including the religious field, is exempt in this litigious society of ours. Being a lifelong student in any field of responsibility may not prevent malpractice, but it will certainly put us on guard to improve our professional practices. Leaders as well as followers pursuing serious continuing education know how necessary and essential good learning is in fulfilling our calling to be competent and trustworthy practitioners.

The first hundred days for a new leader in any organization are of utmost importance, for they set the tone in terms of a leader's character and competence before anyone is willing to place their trust in him or her. For any of us at work, what we say and what we don't say make an impression: "Your actions and language will categorize you as indecisive or authoritarian, fair or arbitrary, a visionary or closed-minded."[7] The so-called honeymoon period, as most new followers and leaders ought to know, is not a function of one's job title but instead depends on the results achieved. If you are truly a lifelong student, your first hundred days will reveal the quality of your listening and speaking as well as your ability to resist the temptation to announce a quick fix as a "solution" to past and present issues. It might be wise to keep most initial assessments to yourself as you listen and observe. Most followers will then accept you as someone who is taking the process of learning seriously. In other words, your careful approach will establish your credibility in modest ways while you learn from all who have been there longer and have suggestions to make. Hopefully, your "student hat" will be with you throughout your tenure in office as your own professional contribution increases with time.

As we emerge in our leadership roles, we need also to be reminded that all the members of the organization have a stake in the enterprise and are entitled to participate in the cultural change of the organization. Management by itself does not change the culture. This was probably one of the most important lessons that Dr. Lawrence Summers learned, unfortunately too late in his case, during his short tenure as president of Harvard University. As Dr. Summers expresses it,

> I didn't have a well-developed theory of what I was doing. . . . I underappreciated the sense in which I was new . . . then I made another mistake. I didn't fully appreciate the importance of simply providing traditional institutional reassurances. By asking and challenging everything, you create a lot of uncertainty, and that

uncertainty can be debilitating to the ongoing functioning of the organization. I failed to appreciate that if you're going to be questioning everybody and challenging everybody, you have to do a lot of reassuring in return. I didn't say, "Isn't Harvard great?"[8]

With hindsight Dr. Summers candidly shares the fact that during his first hundred days in the Harvard presidency, he would have been wise to mention that it was also a new chapter for Harvard and for himself. This could have gained him some empathy and reduced the amount of goodwill capital lost as subsequent events unfolded. In retrospect, he wishes that he had been smarter. I wonder how many other newcomers to leadership positions also share Summers's reflections and wish they could have another chance to relate with colleagues with greater understanding for their situation.

None of us should abandon our student status as lifelong learners who reflect and review the relations between followers and leader in the hope of growing together productively. Professor Ronald A. Heifetz of Harvard University, a leadership expert, insightfully warns us to be aware of the myth of leadership, which lures us into the trap of becoming the lone warrior. This mythic picture of the leader reinforces the isolation the new leader experiences as "the solitary individual whose heroism and brilliance enables him to lead the way."[9] Instead of falling into this situation, the leader's strategic challenge is to give

the work back to people without abandoning them. Overload them and they will avoid learning. Under load them and they will grow too dependent or complacent. Thus, an authority has to bear the weight of problems for a time. This can be a very real burden. Unloading that weight on people unprepared to respond would be negligent. Shouldering the pain and uncertainties of an institution particularly in times of distress comes with the job of authority. It can only be avoided at the institution's peril.[10]

Heifetz then moves on to suggest seven ways for new leadership to bear the responsibility without having to lose effectiveness under the strain:[11]

1. Place yourself on the balcony.
2. Distinguish self from role.
3. Externalize the conflict.
4. Use partners.

5. Listen, using oneself as data.
6. Find a sanctuary.
7. Preserve a sense of purpose.

Heifetz expands on each of these points in his study, which I encourage you to read. Heifetz's point—and what I find crucial from my own experience—is to understand that neither leadership nor followership can be exercised alone. Partners are needed within and without the organization who can appreciate the dynamics involved. I wonder if Summers was aware of Heifetz's books and his expertise on organizational relationships at Harvard. They could have had (and perhaps they did have) informal and private discussions as colleagues before the tension between faculty and president had gone too far.

Speaking for myself, I find Professor Heifetz's leadership wisdom insightful:

> The lone-warrior model of leadership is heroic suicide. Each of us has blind spots that require the vision of others. Each of us has passions that need to be contained by others. Anyone can lose the capacity to get on the balcony, particularly when the pressure mounts. Every person who leads needs help in distinguishing self from role and identifying the underlying issues that generate attack.[12]

In the interactive partnership between leaders and followers, all parties need to alternate between participating and observing, between being active and being reflective. When this happens in partnership, organizations will be recognized for their quality of competence and the team will be empowered to excel.

Next we focus on the importance of a leader's commitment as well as competence throughout the organization, inspiring everyone to take nothing for granted in our common task to succeed. Such an attitude will unite the organization to advance in its journey, especially when the going gets tough.

3
Commitment

Lee Iacocca is the CEO who saved Chrysler in the 1970s. Well known to an older generation of fans for his salesmanship and leadership abilities, he earned friends as well as foes for his candor and business acumen. His 2007 book *Where Have All the Leaders Gone* illustrates his style of leadership. While his book was ranked well on the best-seller list, a critical review in the *Wall Street Journal* by Paul Ingrassia, a Pulitzer Prize winner and vice president of news strategy for Dow Jones at the time, felt otherwise. He concluded his review by saying, "Mr. Iacocca really deserved his hero-celebrity status when he served Chrysler a quarter-century ago. Now he deserves to relax."[1]

Ingrassia's negative judgment did a disservice to Iacocca, who is not the type of person who "retires" from his sense of service to others. I happen to agree with Iacocca's outlook; it points to his enduring sense of commitment and values as a leader. His attitude toward service in relation to compensation has been missing in recent years among a number of leaders who have crippled their reputations as corporate executives before employees and the larger public they serve. Thankfully, there are still many fine executives in the Iacocca tradition, whose values and discipline have kept them from following the slippery road of Enron, WorldCom, and others. Our aim in these pages is to increase the number of dedicated ethical leaders.

Today's public perception of CEOs has been clouded by excesses in compensation and stock options and by a lack of personal transparency.

Iacocca's example raises the paramount question, "Can we ever recover again our confidence in corporate America?" No doubt this factor has contributed to the growing trend of young people in pursuit of establishing their own "ideal" organization. They wish to distance themselves from the prevalent image of corporate America as a place of greed. Such leadership types, according to Iacocca, ought to be led away in handcuffs. He writes,

> Greed is big, but I'm not letting envy off the hook. That's a deadly sin, too. Sometimes I think the real culprit is envy. A CEO looks at another CEO and says, "Hey, he's making fifty million, and I'm only making thirty million. I'm in the same industry, and I'm better than he is. I should be making sixty million." That's how the executives' compensations spiral up. Nobody says, "Well, thirty million is pretty good." So envy can trump greed.[2]

We received a firsthand report on how the pressures can mount in a corporation when Pittsburgh Seminary's Center on Business, Religion, and Public Life invited Enron whistle-blower Sherron S. Watkins to speak at a public gathering. Watkins was vice president at Enron in finance when she informed CEO Kenneth L. Lay in a confidential memo that there was serious trouble in the company. Even though Lay did not openly acknowledge any difficulty to Watkins, he had quietly unloaded seventy million dollars of his own stock in the company while freezing the employees' withdrawals in their pension plans. Ironically, his unexpected death shortly after his trial and conviction for fraud and conspiracy but before his final sentencing caused his conviction to be thrown out. As a result, the seventy million will not, most likely, be recovered for distribution among the pension-poor employees.[3] This whole event is sad. Frankly, we all suffer from such behavior.

Iacocca's book illustrates not only that our values are in disarray but also that the commitment so necessary to an organization's welfare and its benefits to the community have been undermined and need restoration. Iacocca is disturbed by the lack of sacrifice among leaders. He points to the saving of Chrysler in the 1970s as a team effort led by his example of leadership to take a salary cut as CEO and reduce his pay to a symbolic one dollar a year. The leader in an organizational crisis ought to share the sacrifice. "Then," says Iacocca, "I went to the executives and asked them to take a pay cut. Finally, I went to Doug Fraser of the UAW and asked what the union could give. The workers really came through. Over a nineteen-month period, the workers made $25 billion in concessions. It was the workers more than the government loan that saved the company."[4]

The reality today is that the leader's commitment to the organization is expected to be proportionate to the organization's total compensation package. And when is it evident that anyone's higher compensation actually increases performance? An organization under pressure expects greater effort from everyone without necessarily raising anyone's compensation for a while. Such a response needs to be transparent to the entire organization. In a crisis, stock options can be an incentive for CEOs and others in management to assert themselves under pressure. Is this the wisest way to operate? Today, CEOs expect added dollars even if the company performs poorly, thereby further demoralizing the organization. Actual leadership results and the compensation package ought to make sense to the personnel, its board, and shareholders, all of whom are stakeholders in the process and outcome.

According to J. Richard Finlay, founder of the Centre for Corporate and Public Governance, salary itself can actually be a miniscule component of CEO compensation and largely irrelevant within the larger context of stock options and perks that are awarded. Some of these factors are not transparent to the members of the organization and the public at large. In discovering this practice shareholders and boards of directors are now raising serious questions on behalf of the organization's morale, all in an effort to secure public support for the company's value to the wider community. But is anything truly happening to keep rampant CEO salaries in check?[5]

More recently, executive compensation issues came under fire with banks, investment brokers, and AIG bailout discussions. Another trend is also hopefully emerging today among undergraduate and graduate business classrooms to create a new generation of committed CEOs who are more approachable and whose future leadership styles will be subject to closer examination. Organizations as well as the public expect a more meaningful level of commitment from leaders to indicate that company morale matters and will benefit everyone, not only those who anticipate stock options and so forth. The object is to develop a more interconnected spirit of commitment that will impact the organization positively, for it is clear that rewards such as stock options and other monetary incentives in themselves will not create for leaders and followers a unified spirit of togetherness throughout the organization. Everyone need not receive the same compensation, but everyone's talents and efforts should be appropriately acknowledged.

Today's leaders must define themselves by meaningful measurements that are transparent to all who are associated with the organization. This offers a believable identity to one's character and commitment within and without the organization. Such an example was clearly evident in the leadership style that Iacocca projected.

Followers and supporters of organizations need a leader with a style of commitment they are inspired to emulate in their lives. Without authentic mutual commitments, leaders and followers will "burn out" in their relationships with one another. Some may choose early retirement to pursue a second or third career, like attending seminary classes for inner growth, followed by serving in a church, teaching in a public school, working in a social agency, or traveling abroad to assist some remote community in need. Through such ventures, a growing number are experiencing a rekindling of their passion to serve at a time when others are struggling to find purpose in their lives.

The Bible informs us, however, that God never gives up on us when we are willing to pursue a divine purpose for our lives (Ps. 138:8). Have you ever had the need to renew your sense of purpose in life? You may be nearing the threshold of a new venture that will revive your spirit and imagination, but you may not yet be willing to acknowledge publicly the direction of your thoughts. Together, we may even be questioning why God hasn't given up on us while others have. Whatever the case, we may be presently in the process of uncovering the larger reality that serving others is the key that unlocks one's vitality, encouraging us to engage in risk taking within our present organization or to move on to something new.

CONSIDER LEADERSHIP AND FOLLOWERSHIP AS SPIRITUAL CALLINGS

One's vocational calling may undergo a number of turns during one's lifetime. We must always be alert to unexpected opportunities for new forms of service. God's guidance may well direct us to new adventures that surprise and lead us to unexpected and exciting relationships, appearing like a promised rainbow that refreshes and renews us for the next steps in our lives. Unless we nurture spiritual qualities in our journey of faith, we will soon find ourselves without purpose. My working hypothesis in life is that sustainable and creative leadership is nurtured and maintained by a renewed awakening of faith, hope, and love in our everyday lives. Unfortunately the term "spirituality" is often misunderstood and cheapened in current religious and secular conversations. We need to discern the nature of authentic spiritual direction through careful and critical assessment, with the aid of knowledgeable mentors and prayerful reflection.

The wisdom of sound leadership will acknowledge our finiteness and limitations. Surprises and miscalculations are inevitable. Decision making is never a perfect science, no matter how much we maximize the information available to us before we act. Wise leadership is also mindful of everyone's vulnerability and the possibilities of failure. In all humility, we need to acknowledge to ourselves the gap that exists between divine intention and our human interpretations and execution of the plan ahead.

Outstanding leadership has at its core a built-in quality of humility. We become arrogant if we fail to acknowledge the presence of divine grace in our decisions; a genuine humility is the mark of true spirituality. With a successful outcome, we seem to ignore or forget the nurturing path in faith, hope, and love that sustains us, especially when the odds are stacked against us and "the right" outcome seems impossible. Authentic humility never forgets where the credit goes, and those inspired by the leader's humility are empowered.

At times we are stubborn and too sure of ourselves, and thinking that we are always right can cause misfortune to ourselves and our organization. Spiritually oriented leadership, on the other hand, avoids equating one's own personal agendas with the divine will. Once we are aware of our biases, we are less tempted to fall back on religious, political, social, and economic programs to justify our limited understanding of complex situations. Means and ends do influence each other in the final shape of any outcome. There is often an unseen divide between the infinite and the finite, between the absolute and the relative, between human and divine understandings. We may all reflect the divine image, but our actions do not necessarily guarantee that a divine standard will be maintained in our practice of justice and mercy. Somewhere in the mix, our self-interest buries the thorny issues facing us.

During our periods of conflict, we need to maintain a spirit of openness with trepidation and hope, seeking divine guidance with every step. Here is where we need to grasp the message found in Proverbs 1:7: "The fear of the LORD is the beginning of knowledge." In other words, we need an attitude of respect, humility, and patience to ascertain what the divine leading might be in any given situation. When we are faithfully humble before God, we will be entrusted and blessed with wisdom that influences and directs the outcome of our decision-making process. During this period of discernment, we need to maintain a degree of tentativeness before any action is taken; otherwise we will be unable to grasp the message of the text in Proverbs.

Understanding the nature of divine wisdom can have a positive impact on today's global society. First, such wisdom gives us the capacity to listen with our hearts as well as with our heads, enabling us to be intuitive, insightful, and dependent on divine leading. This ability is essential, I believe, for sustainable leadership to thrive under pressure. Because the essence of leadership lies in making good choices, it normally entails some measure of risk taking. Leaders are often called on to act in critical moments in a way that can have either a positive or negative impact on one's institution or organization, as well as on national policy. No doubt, there will be uncharted waters and pathways ahead.

Leaders wishing to succeed will listen carefully to many voices (like King Solomon) but reserve themselves in prayer to choose wisely. Leadership decisions are not based solely on the data at hand but also on the ability to anticipate the unpredictable consequences that face us.

Now we can better understand why King Solomon was strongly motivated before his enthronement to pray for the gift of wisdom rather than power, wealth, fame, or even the destruction of his enemies. Aware of his limitations, he knew the importance of having the gift of wisdom. And God was pleased, granting him not only wisdom but prosperity as well. So equipped, Solomon was quickly tested on how effective he would be as a leader. You may recall the story as told in 1 Kings 3:3–28. Two women are clinging to a recently born infant, each claiming to be the child's true mother. King Solomon is asked to decide between the two claims. He knows everyone in the king's chamber is watching. How should the newly installed king respond? He reaches for a sword to split the baby in half, apparently intending to give one half of the baby to each woman who claims the infant child. Immediately, the true mother speaks up. "Spare the child and give him to the other woman," she says. Solomon understands the cry of the true mother, who wishes to save her child, whatever the outcome. The King responds by returning the child to her. Have you wondered, as I have, whether Solomon would have actually carried out his threat to cut the baby in two, or was he simply bluffing?

Most leaders know from experience that they can't afford to bluff; they must be willing to act. Otherwise, there is the danger of losing

7/12

From the desk of…
PHIL CALIAN

Dear Jeanne,

From one spiritual leader (my Dad)
to another (you).
I hope all is going well
at Mayo.

With much love,

Jill & Phil

531 Cruyaauta Rd.
Pittsburgh 15215

(312) 506-6490
pcalian@wavelandinvestments.com

one's credibility. The gift of wisdom provided Solomon with the intuitive insight to look ahead to the consequences of his decision before he carried it out. Herein lies a major aspect of wisdom—namely, to have hindsight before the event. Each of us knows that anyone can be a Monday-morning quarterback and perhaps improve on the decisions of Sunday's football game. However, a wise quarterback or leader is one who has the foresight to understand the outcome before executing the decision. Possessing divine wisdom is at the heart of spiritual leadership that is driven by faith, hope, and love for the lives of those so dependent on the outcome of the situation at stake.

Michael and Sandy Lee Maccoby are gifted professionals with many talents. Sandy Lee is a teacher, author, and artist, and Michael is a psychoanalyst and leadership specialist well known through his writing and counseling. I can recall on our visits to the Maccoby home the hand-painted plaque in their dining room that expresses in the different languages of the world the spiritual wisdom of the ages, namely, the well-known Golden Rule: "Do unto others as you would have them do unto you." This wisdom is not limited to any single religious tradition. Stated in various ways, it essentially calls us to exercise respect for one another's intrinsic worth, transcending the self-centeredness that often obscures one's awareness of the rights and needs of others.

The Golden Rule is centered on the religious belief that everyone is created in God's image and we are therefore expected to respect that divine image in one another, no matter how tarnished it may appear. Practicing its intent is another way of expressing faith, hope, and love in relationship with one another. The Golden Rule can be seen as an introduction into its wider meaning outlined in the Ten Commandments, directing us to uphold the divine image within us and to keep human life human. Leadership that practices the spiritual qualities of faith, hope, and love embedded in the Golden Rule will have a framework for abiding peace and goodwill in our fragmented world, with its divided allegiances.

In short, the spiritual side of leadership envisions faith, hope, and love operating together as a leadership style to sustain us in all circumstances that threaten to rob us of our humanity, whatever the expedient justification for doing so might be. Praying for the gift of Solomon's wisdom and exercising the Golden Rule will provide the foundation for sustainable leadership among organizations within an ever-changing global society.

DEDICATE YOURSELF TO YOUR PRIMARY MISSION: KNOW THE DIFFERENCE BETWEEN SKIRMISHES AND BATTLES

Commitment is nurtured by our spiritual roots. It clarifies the abiding purpose and rationale that give strength to our organizations and institutions. Where are we today? Are we still on track or have we been derailed organizationally and professionally? Has our primary mission lost its meaning, and are we afraid to admit that fact? We can't take our commitment for granted or accept organizational decline as normal for the times. Strategic planning among profit and nonprofit organizations requires us to ask continually the hard questions. For example, has our focus become too narrow, too self-serving, and as a result, too boring to many of us? Reviewing ourselves regularly is necessary if we are to maintain our creative edge critically and constructively in order to make positive contributions to society. To be complacent is to become confused about our mission as we slip into inaction. Have we lost the zest behind our message and mission as an organization? Are we repeating ourselves too often with clichés? Are we only hearing echoes without results?

When honest with ourselves, we may find we are preoccupied with doubts over our organizational and personal goals in life. Somewhere along the way, we may have lost interest in our institution's mission; perhaps our nation's faith in itself and in its responsibilities to others is also lost. When all rhetoric is put aside, we are actually interested only in self-survival. Heroes are nice, but that's not the real message we want our children and grandchildren to hear. This prevailing feeling of being disconnected is perhaps due to our fatigue with local and global conflicts, or it may simply be that we have unanswered vocational questions still stirring within us. We may wonder if we have chosen the wrong path and fear any change at this point in our lives.

The London Business School uncovered this growing factor of anxiety among its recent graduates—especially younger management executives who felt the need to return for further schooling. Graduate and continuing education courses highlighted the tension felt by these young executives as they undertook strategic transformation changes in their organizations. In classroom discussions, participants mentioned that past practices in traditional organizations have masked the inertia that exists, making it more difficult for risk and change to take place. This situation affects almost everyone directly and indirectly these days. Many thus feel disconnected in today's rapidly changing context. Similar circumstances also occur among long-standing nonprofit organizations being challenged by the rise of megachurches, new social enterprises, and the rising tide of social entrepreneurs working more innovatively to enlarge their outreach to the needy and help them to raise financial resources for the benefit of their communities.

In the midst of this growing anxiety, the London Business School has now expanded its analysis to include a session on managing personal commitments within the context of change and future service for organizations faced with unclear paths ahead. Business schools and other graduate professional programs are realizing increasingly that personal commitments are also tied to individual belief systems and expectations; this tends to be particularly true among nonprofits but also among people-oriented organizations. All these factors influence behavioral attitudes among employees as well as volunteers.

Perhaps profits and nonprofits should team up and design a course of action for all followers and leaders seeking a better relationship of goodwill to enhance their common need for meaningful purpose. As they work together within their new organizational structures, those who are turned on purposefully together will contribute far more in transforming organizations to serve the public good. Teamwork will benefit relationships with supporters, clients, and the larger community in their varied needs.

If we are indeed dedicated to transforming organizations and ourselves in the process, we will quickly find that the task is not easy. This fact is well known to consultants, teachers, and managers of change. Those who work hard on transforming themselves and their organizations are often underappreciated. This is discouraging because there is a common hope to improve communities through the organizations we serve. Teamwork is required; every step forward is work, and every step backward calls for heightened motivation for the team to turn the tide. Inertia exists in every community seeking to uncover its turning point toward its rainbow of hope. Resistance is expressed well in the French cliché "Plus ca change, plus c'est la meme chose" (The more things change, the more they stay the same).

One important key for successful change is how leaders exemplify their commitment to inspire empowerment and confidence within the organization. There is a widespread misconception of empowerment in many organizations. Throughout my years as president of an educational institution, my colleagues and staff often assumed that I was the only one who was empowered to act. How wrong they were!

Frankly, I shared with fellow colleagues how powerless I felt at times, far more often than they would expect. The subject of empowerment raises many questions based on our current confusion and understanding of governance, not only in the halls of learning but also among corporations faced with issues of truth telling and compensation/ financial matters within the organization. See the timely book by Professor John C. Coffee Jr., director of the Center on Corporate Governance at Columbia University Law School, titled *Gatekeepers: The Professions and Corporate Governance*. The difference between "nobodies" and "somebodies" often breaks down to salary matters and issues of equity within organizations. The soul of a healthy organization emerges through good communication in sensitive matters of salary when these are discussed wisely and openly, revealing how responsibility and performance are related.

In a time when CEO compensation has skyrocketed compared to that of other workers, the disparity raises more often than not a significant morale barrier for team building and transformation within organizations. The new class of celebrities is no longer limited to professional athletes and movie personalities; CEOs and fund executives have joined that inner circle. CEOs, on average, as reported in the Congressional Research Service records, earn 179 times as much as lower-rank workers, double the 90 to 1 ratio in 1984, according to the agency's calculations. Such a gap makes it difficult for any CEO to impress the organization's personnel facing the challenges of change, even when the leader's new salary might be only a token one dollar a year plus large stock options, with millions already received.

The current compensation discussions are also related to empowerment issues in organizations, according to Michael Maccoby in a recent article, "ReThinking Empowerment."[6] The conflict has been heightened by the impact of technology. As we know, organizational life is rapidly changing, requiring the rethinking of empowerment for employees, shareholders, and clients.

Today, empowerment means both delegating power and responding to demand, and to execute either side of empowerment calls for accepting responsibility and accountability as well as their consequences. It is in this latter aspect that empowerment and governance fall short of our expectations. Empowerment may sound like a zero-sum game, says Maccoby, "meaning if they get more power, you will have less. There are two kinds of power: power over, meaning authority, and power to, meaning enablement."[7] The aim of followers and leaders is to transform one another's demands into a fresh way of coming together to improve the quality of dialogue so that everyone benefits, enabling the organization to move forward. For empowerment to work effectively, all interested parties within the organization need to be well informed about what is at stake with its present governance and what is needed when all parties work together to achieve organizational goals and mutual well-being. To create an empowered organization or institution, says Maccoby, "you need a learning organization (community) where people gain knowledge about the business, customer needs, what creates profit (or resources for nonprofits) as well as learning from their mistakes."[8] Many organizations, I believe, can benefit from Maccoby's insights.

Reaching an organization's primary mission in a changing world will require informed conversation with all interested parties. Such conversations can help cultivate the cultural soil needed to stimulate trust and nurture a culture of enlightened persuasion. At the heart of persuasion is an understanding that enables us to accept and take action. Without the power of persuasion, our hope for any purposeful turnaround hasn't a chance of succeeding.

Paul Levy's story about the turnaround at Beth Israel Deaconess Medical Center is an excellent illustration of how the process of enlightened persuasion can empower and transform all parties involved. Harvard professors David A. Garvin and Michael A. Roberto describe it in a helpful article that identifies the process and issues for us.[9] Levy's story illustrates the toughest task awaiting followers and leaders seeking organizational transformation. Their challenge is to avoid those backsliding practices that lead to dysfunctional routines as they confront the following:

1. A culture of "no" that resists change
2. Dog-and-pony shows—the authors of the Levy article call it "death by PowerPoint."
3. Efforts to change the main subject being discussed
4. End runs, described as "After the meeting ends, debate begins"
5. "Analysis-paralysis" to avoid a definitive decision
6. "This too shall pass—a heads-down bunker mentality"

While being mindful of the dysfunctional games that are played, the change-team at Beth Israel focused on "The Four Phases of a Persuasion Campaign,"[10] in which an implementation followed the developmental stage in order to bring clarity to the organization's wish to enhance its mission. The persuasion process included the following important steps:

Announce plan.

Phase 1—Convince employees that radical change is imperative; demonstrate why the new direction is the right one.

Phase 2—Position and frame preliminary plan; gather feedback; announce final plan.

Phase 3—Manage employee mood through consistent communication.

Phase 4—Reinforce behavioral guidelines to avoid backsliding.

Turnaround Process: Develop plan/implementation process.

Proceeding from personal commitment to the organization's betterment requires a good deal of energy and time. It is thus important to distinguish skirmishes from battles on the way to reaching one's goal. In many organizations, too much effort is often spent in minor skirmishes, which leaves little energy to confront the status quo of decline in the organization and its future within the larger community it serves. Any organization preoccupied with surface skirmishes will fail to bring significant transformation to its personnel and programs. In short, skirmishes only divide organizations to the detriment of their primary mission.

NURTURE YOUR PASSION; CONQUER SELF-PITY

Self-pity at times runs through our skirmishes and adds to our feelings of unfulfillment, which explains in part why we think we are nobodies and why we fail to develop a more positive frame of mind. Instead of harboring this demoralizing feeling of nothingness, we need to review our attitudes and overcome any negativity vis-á-vis our more basic concern for the organization's improvement. Together we need to determine whose interest is best served by the current status quo and agree on what conditions need to be changed. Accepting a satisfactory meaning to our lives cannot be forced on us, nor will it simply be handed to us; we need to nurture a purposeful passion that promotes the community's well-being, driven by our common commitments and a caring spirit. True identity, as John Gardner has indicated, is built on having common trust and acting on commitments, "whether the commitment is to your religion, to an ethical order, to your life work, to loved ones, to the common good or to coming generations."[11]

We need to face the future with our eyes wide open to changing realities and with the passion to do what is right, whatever the strong resistance before us might be. It pays for us to reserve a touch of naiveté even as we act boldly, defying the many voices telling us to "play it safe" when confronted with a situation that needs correcting. Oftentimes, a safe attitude borders on complacency and caution as we avoid the transformation and improvement required by the situation.

Normally followers and leaders desiring change need to agree to pay the price of discernment. There is no escaping the fact that "playing it safe" is not always right. This, no doubt, was evident in the American spirit that prevailed in 1776. Understanding this harsh reality is difficult and no doubt explains why many potential leaders remain undeveloped, having lost their true identity and fulfillment in life.

According to the Center for Creative Leadership, 40 percent of new CEOs fail in their first eighteen months in office, and the turnover is rising. "In a 2002 study, the Center found that the number of CEOs leaving their jobs had increased 10 percent since 2001."[12] Challenger, Gray, and Christmas, Inc. reports that the greatest challenge within corporate America is finding replacements for CEOs. Perhaps this explains, in part, the stratospheric rise in compensation practices for leaders even when the performance is mediocre.

The average tenure of presidents in higher education (universities, colleges, seminaries, etc.) oscillates between four and eight years, and as with corporate CEOs the replacement prospects are not as great as most institutions would like to see. What profit and nonprofit organization's desire is the greater supply of leaders that author Jim Collins refers to as "Level 5 Leadership."[13] Based on a five-year research project, Collins believes the key ingredient organizations are seeking in leaders is a personal combination of genuine humility and a committed professional will to succeed.

Collins is not looking for the bigger-than-life charismatic types but for a kind of person who can transform an organization "from good to great," one possessing all the qualities from Levels 1 to 4 but still embodying those of a Level 5 leader. One such example is Darwin Smith, who led the remarkable transformation of Kimberly-Clark Corp. into a consumer-paper-products business. At his retirement celebration, Smith modestly reflected on his exceptional performance by simply saying, "I never stopped trying to become qualified for the job."[14]

The Level 5 hierarchy is as follows: Level 1 is the highly capable individual who has the skills and spirit to work hard; Level 2 is the contributing team member who works well with others; Level 3 is the competent manager who organizes people and resources well; Level 4 is the effective leader who is a catalyst for commitment to a compelling vision that stimulates a high-performance standard; and Level 5 manifests overall a personal humility and professional will that inspires colleagues and customers to support the organization. For our discussion and further reflection Collins outlines for us the yin and yang of Level 5 leadership as follows: [15]

Personal Humility	Professional Will
Demonstrates a compelling modesty, shunning public adulation, never boastful.	Creates superb results, a clear catalyst in the transition from good to great.
Acts with quiet, calm determination; relies principally on inspired standards, not inspiring charisma to motivate.	Demonstrates an unwavering resolve to do whatever must be done to produce the best long-term results, no matter how difficult.
Channels ambition into the company, not the self; sets up successors for even more greatness in the next generation.	Sets the standard of building an enduring great company; will settle for nothing less.
Looks in the mirror, not out the window, to apportion responsibility for poor results, never blaming other people, external factors, or bad luck.	Looks out the window, not in the mirror, to apportion credit for the success of the company—to other people, external factors, and good luck.

Collins' Level 5 leadership has many of the qualities of Robert Greenleaf's servant-leader model, which is known to a wide range of leaders. From my perspective (and perhaps also for Collins) it appears that the Level 5 leader manifests a spiritual height to leadership in the marketplace that blends followership and leadership as the yin and yang, directing us to participate in the exciting transformation of an organization's contribution beyond itself to the community at large. [16]

Next on our agenda is the importance of the leader's character and its role in the transformation of the organization. The leader's character can also influence followers to become leaders who in turn become true listeners who hear what's being said. In short, the leader's character has an enduring impact on the standards of the organization before its public, touching countless lives with its message, products, and services.

4

Character

Everyone can be a "character" of a sort, but to whom do we reserve the honorific designation "a person of good character," one who is wise and caring? One such person was Abraham Lincoln, known as "honest Abe." How will others frame your "character"? Any useful evaluation of a person's lifestyle and moral behavior approximates one's true character, a quality hopefully admired by followers, peers, and even strangers.

Perhaps another way to understand character is to trace a person's inherent traits—the dynamic that goes on within us, consisting of our unspoken words, feelings, habits, and afterthoughts—an unwritten internalized diary, so to speak, that we are constantly constructing and recomposing as we react to external events and relationships. This internal dynamic helps shape a person's character and influences the development of one's public persona and its impact for good or ill on the lives of others. The many books on Abraham Lincoln's life and legacy have highlighted this developmental factor in the shaping of his character. Even today, scholars continue to study the traits behind his leadership, authenticity, and remarkable message. What quality traits do you admire most in someone of good character?

TRUST: THE TRAIT THAT MUST BE EARNED

Transforming an organization demands an assessment of the leader's character and ability to motivate employees and volunteers to share common goals and responsibilities within the organization. Every effort to gain public trust depends on the efforts of the organization's entire personnel. The leader who wishes to make a positive difference knows this. In due course the company's record of dependability and character enhances its public image and self-esteem. The organization also gains credibility. Followers and leaders learn quickly that the characteristic of trust can never be taken for granted. It needs to be earned on a daily basis. Building trust is an unending task that reflects one's behavior, which is constantly under pressure. The temptation is to compromise standards and to take shortcuts, often leading to unwise outcomes.

Character is more than the total sum of good traits seen in one's honesty, caring, reliability, fairness, straight talk, and consistency in lifestyle. These attributes are certainly significant and necessary steps toward building character and trust, but are they sufficient in themselves?

Achieving total trust in an organization through the lifestyle of its leaders and personnel may not be possible nor realistic, given the harsh realities and negative publicity often encountered unexpectedly by organizations.[1] None of us lives in a perfect utopia as sometimes depicted in an idealized travelogue. We all live "east of Eden," whether we are willing to admit it or not, and we can never escape the imperfect conditions of our human existence. Nonetheless, striving for human trust is a worthy goal if we wish to enjoy healthy, fulfilling relationships. In any case, we need to pause from time to time and ask ourselves how satisfactory our present view of reality is and what we can realistically do to improve it.

My own reality picture is as follows: I find myself living in a context of imperfect persons who make imperfect decisions in an imperfect world. I find myself belonging to this global sphere of reality every day of my life. In other words, no one is perfect wherever they live. Living in a world that expects perfection may not be paradise for anyone. It is within this context of reality that we need to examine our values, the quality of our own personal character, and the level of trust we are willing to maintain and practice with one another.

Upholding an adequate level of trustworthiness is a never-ending task in a multicultural world, where diversity is desirable. It is necessary to have followers and leaders who understand their limitations and imperfections within our global context if we are to welcome and tolerate human diversity and enable persons of all backgrounds to succeed. Lifelong learning requires us to earn one another's trust locally and globally through an endless series of encounters. The task of learning to live together involves hard work as well as a forgiving spirit.

Given our earthly realities and vicissitudes, there is little chance that any of us can survive without practicing a caring spirit toward one another. This is the way we uphold our common humanity and its limitations. The practice of good character is dedicated to this end; global welfare envisions us working together, which in turn requires listening with patience in the midst of our torturous misunderstandings. Trusting or mistrusting those we encounter will speak volumes to the level of health or malady in our shared life together. Living well in a global society requires mutual accountability worldwide from everyone. It also calls for humility from rich and poor toward each other.

At the present time, unfortunately, we are contributing to each other's anxiety around the world. None of us, it appears, is safe; we are driven by an expanding nuclear-oriented world. The result is fear mixed with national pride, as nations seek to be included in the circle of countries that can create a nuclear cloud. In short, nuclear dangers abound in today's world. The international population yearns for believable stories from caring leaders who truly wish to defuse the existing towers of Babel that foster distrust, suspicions, and a false illusion of security at the expense of the other's insecurity. We cannot afford to be parochial in these life-threatening matters. Haven't the past one-hundred-plus years of wars taught us anything? Our present experiences with globalization inform us that we are indeed living in a restless, crowded, and insecure world where so-called secure boundaries are also an illusion. "Feeling safe" is likewise an illusion when we are globally awake. Today's international Babel is moving us backward rather than forward; most conversations about peacemaking fall sadly on deaf ears as our hatred of one another mounts, based on past memories and present confusion.

Professor Howard Gardner of Harvard University, in his thoughtful and helpful book *Leading Minds: An Anatomy of Leadership*,[2] explains that leaders tell stories to show how they understand the world, revealing their character and grasp of the situation. These stories reveal the true identity and passion of the leader, suggesting his or her level of tolerance for ambiguity and manipulation. Stories show the leader's tenacity in maintaining authenticity before followers. In short, listing the leader's qualities of character may in itself not be sufficient to mirror one's true style of leadership and intent. Instead, the reaction of followers may be a better index in revealing the leader's real intent.

Just as followers want trusted leaders, leaders themselves search for trusting followers. However, the desire for trusted partners can lead us to isolated and parochial outcomes if we are unwilling to hear the lonely voice advising us to take the necessary risk that might heal strained relationships or pursue new directions that have more promise. General George C. Marshall prevailed as a useful and exemplary commanding officer during World War II and after the war through the Marshall Plan for the recovery of Europe. He succeeded because he spoke his mind and told the truth as he saw it. The temptation for followers is often to remain with the "yes chorus" without expressing dissent.

Many of us, I suspect, would like to practice more trust but do not because our confidences have been betrayed. We have no intention of getting burned again. Maybe this is why we stand aside when serious decisions and actions are made. Some choose to be loners, wary of potential conflicts. Trust building is always a process of risk taking; it includes the need to practice forgiveness frequently, especially if the betrayal of confidentiality happens again, which it will.

True forgiveness is a constant learning experience, educating ourselves to the fact that we cannot forget the past with its scars. With time, we learn that most caring and loving relationships require an ongoing process of learning to forgive without forgetting, whatever the errors or tragedies might have been. Practicing forgiveness is a tough business. Human societies around the world can be largely unforgiving. The power of forgiveness shown by the Amish in Pennsylvania over the killing of their schoolchildren in 2006 caught our attention and flagged our own shortcomings. (See the film on the subject produced by Martin Doblmeier, *The Power of Forgiveness*, released in 2007. Doblmeier is also known for his acclaimed film about Dietrich Bonhoeffer.)

I wonder at times how many battles and broken relationships could have been avoided if the painful practice of forgiveness had been our prevailing style of behavior. The Swiss theologian and professor Hans Kung was quite insightful in his public presentations when he indicated that we can't have peace among the nations of the world until we have peace among the religions of the world. If religious followers can't practice a measure of forgiveness among themselves as taught in their respective faiths, how can we expect forgiveness among nations? I don't know of any religion, including Christianity, that doesn't need to practice greater forgiveness within its own family of followers as well as with its neighbors of other faiths and those who deny any belief at all.

Whenever trust has been lost, it is difficult to regain. This is true between followers and leaders in organizations as it is among nations and religious institutions. It seems all parties who hold grudges are

carrying heavy baggage from their past that greatly influences their present attitudes and prevents new beginnings. Where is the spiritual rebirth
and willingness that will enable us to alter our attitudes, honor the fallen
heroes of our nations, and bring about a healthier transformed future for
which they shed their lives? What has happened to our willingness to
be creative risk takers? How can we learn to ask new questions instead
of burying ourselves under repetitive clichés? Such fearful behaviors
prevent us from having any possibility of meaningful peacemaking on
whatever grounds—politically, religiously, and socially.

Without a creative willingness to embrace a new highway of peacemaking, we become prisoners to a past that we can't change. The only
way to honor the memories of the past at a deeper level of understanding and reconciliation for all sides is to free ourselves from narrow
imprisonments of blame and allow ourselves to forgive without forgetting the loss of others' lives for us. Human societies need to build healing roads of reconciliation and hope that point us to a better future. We
need to build constructively on our diversity, rather than wage endless
wars of hostility and genocide that repeat the hatred, suspicion, and
bloodshed of the past.

SENSITIVITY: LISTENING TO HUMAN NEEDS

We recognize that building trust is a never-ending process because
human conflicts are seemingly inevitable and unending. This trust process therefore calls for sensitivity to our surroundings and careful attention to human needs. Ours is not a perfect world as we progress from
childhood through adulthood. Not only do we need to renew our trust
in one another regularly; we also need to understand what trust offers
and doesn't offer in addressing our concerns. It's quite similar to the
child who asks the parents repeatedly, "Do you love me?" The child
always needs assurance of love, especially after being corrected for doing
something wrong. We want to hear that we are still loved in spite of our
errors. We desire such love to be expressed constantly, whatever our age.
So it is with our hunger to have loving trust in our relationships.

We always seem to have excuses for our wrongdoing, whether justi-
fied or otherwise. Trust keeping among humans, like promise keeping,
is never absolute. We do err and ought to seek forgiveness if we are
being honest with ourselves. To forgive and be forgiven is essential if
"covenants of trust" are to restore and maintain our divine and human

relationships. The trust process calls for constant review and honest confessions about strained or broken relationships. We need to exercise spiritual discipline to confront our uncontrolled egos when conflicted anger within can destroy us.

In practicing trust, critically and realistically, we must be consciously mindful of the various types of trust that exist. For instance, there is *simple trust*, discussed in a recent book by Robert C. Solomon and Fernando Flores, *Building Trust: In Business, Politics, Relationships and Life*.[3] Simple trust begins in human infancy but can fail to mature as life becomes more complicated, and it is characterized by a certain innocence, which is often shocked by painful betrayals. Unable to cope, a person can develop inflated expressions of simple trust that lead to unhealthy effects with long-term negative consequences. Simple trust reflects a limited understanding of human nature; it does not process well the actual realities and disappointments informing us that we are living "east of Eden." Simple trust often gives way to cynicism or at least skepticism. As we enter adulthood we adopt "cordial hypocrisy," which often permeates social gatherings and encounters. Within cordial hypocrisy the distinction between etiquette and ethics becomes confused; lying becomes acceptable and normative. As a result, we become less and less trusting and trustworthy to one another. Such an attitude influences and shapes our character.

As we move from simple trust and its consequences, we long for a more meaningful level of trust. Our lives are clearly diminished if we do not belong to some network of trust in relationships. Small groups held together by common interests can provide networks of trust. In order to succeed, networks of trust require an openness and sensitivity to one another's stories. Such sharing is actually an exercise into one's vulnerability. We can't be pushed into it; we need to respect each person's freedom for privacy and practice sensitivity that suspends judgment. Like Jesus with the woman at the well (John 4:7–26), we need to be accepting of persons as we listen to their life stories. Such an approach will take us beyond simple trust to *critical trust*, leading hopefully to an *authentic trust* centered in God, which is the goal in most religious traditions.

We must never forget when we extend trust to others that we are constantly at risk. A negative experience can be devastating, but to stop trusting is worse yet and can lead to despair. In short, life without trusting relationships undermines spiritual, social, and emotional health. Without authentic trust, we would miss one of God's most fulfilling gifts—the experience of taking human journeys together in the spirit of faith, hope, and love, clearly focused on upholding one another.

Finally, there will be those among us who are not willing to engage in this tough process of critical trusting that leads to authentic trust. Some will opt for *blind trust*—a fool's paradise. Blind trust should not be confused with faith or "the leap of faith" as expressed in religious literature. Instead, blind trust is an expression of denial—an attempt to cover up or bury past hurts and betrayals found in authoritarian communities or nations that insist on uniformity. Joining such a controlled gathering is a journey into self-deception in spite of the religious symbolism and pseudopiety that often abounds in such organizations. Communities of blind trust have fixed expectations and rules within a restrictive atmosphere that promises false security but leads to a loss of freedom. Jim Jones' People's Temple and the Branch Davidians are two tragic examples of blind trust; and so were the regimes of Hitler, Stalin, Mao, and others. Blind trust is not the way to a more fulfilling and liberating life.

To sum up, Solomon and Flores have helpfully highlighted for us several dimensions of trust, their limitations, and the significance of forgiveness in relationships. Simple trust is unrealistic in our complex world. Blind trust denies us freedom and is ultimately self-deceptive. Adult trust is critically discerning and rooted in an authentic and caring trust that is divinely based; it can be found in many religious traditions where grace and mercy abound. Authentic trust is realistic and redemptive; it addresses the disappointing realities of betrayal and broken promises but also invites us to risk again and again, propelled by divine forgiveness and its healing power to restore relationships. The scars from the past remind us that we have been liberated from the demons of distrust that tend to resurface when trust is discarded or taken for granted in our organizations and communities.

CREDIBILITY: THE FUSION OF CONFIDENCE AND HUMILITY

Credibility, like trust building, is constantly challenged, misunderstood, and tested by the general public, as well as among followers and friends of any organization. Since perfect trust is beyond our grasp, given our imperfect lives, its presence in an organization demands a leader who can nurture it in a spirit of confidence and humility.

There are many barriers to trust within an organization. Arrogance as well as ignorance, misplaced pride, uncontrolled egos, and misinformed expectations all undermine trusting relations and create suspicion and mistrust. If leaders and followers bear in mind the importance of the organization's mission and service to others and acknowledge their dependence on each other's teamwork, they will also be conscious that we are all sustained by divine grace and mercy. We are expected to pursue our task with excellence and loving care. To assist us in this process we are invited to exercise humor and gratitude at our tasks. The practice of wholesome humor also reminds us not to take ourselves too seriously. We are all subject to a divine destiny that is unfolding daily and whose goals we strive to reach through faith, hope, and love. Herein lies my confidence, whatever the pressures might be.

I am reminded of one of my graduate professors, the famous Karl Barth at the University of Basel in Switzerland, who exemplified humility and humor in his teaching style. His example influenced us doctoral students as well as his wider circle of followers internationally who were aware of his books and ecumenical leadership. "I am not in favor of Barthian theologians," he would say, even though some of us thought he would be flattered by such attention. Professor Barth was not stimulated by those who simply repeated his teachings without thinking for themselves. He preferred to have doctoral students who were independent and critical thinkers. He would regularly laugh at himself, illustrating to the rest of us the confidence he had in his interpretation of the faith and his willingness to be a "critical student" in listening to others. He was also very generous in giving encouragement to his students after every seminar session, by indicating how much he had learned from them and by acknowledging how many unanswered questions he still held for the next time.

I can still recall the time after one seminar session when Barth said to the class that he was helped by the discussion that afternoon, which was based on my seminar paper that week. I frankly wondered to myself, "How could Barth have learned anything from my paper?" I was no more than a beginning graduate student; in other words, an academic nobody. His own genuine sense of humility was illustrated to us many times in spite of the fact that he appeared on the cover of *Time* that year as one of the most distinguished theologians of the twentieth century. Through his example he demonstrated the fusion of confidence, humility, and humor as a credible style of leadership. Like Barth, leaders of any rank in an organization who are able to fuse together and emulate confidence, humility, and humor will go far in advancing trust and learning in the organization. Such leaders can create an inclusive spirit where everyone present can feel that they too are truly somebody, connected to a learning community where mutual trust exists and everyone is respected.

Professor Barth's leadership relates well to the advice from the distinguished management guru Professor Peter Drucker, who has reminded us that organizations, whether profit or nonprofit, "are no longer built on force but on trust. The existence of trust between people does not necessarily mean that they like one another. It means that they understand one another. Taking responsibility for relationships is therefore an absolute necessity."[4] All relationships in any organization are important and need to be valued by leaders and followers alike. There are no nobodies in an organization that aims, whatever its task, to function as a learning community, faithfully and effectively fulfilling its mission while nurturing persons to practice the quality of character that it projects both internally and externally.

Good character is rooted and demonstrated by our trustworthiness and is nurtured daily through skillful and sensitive listening to one another. Careful listening is obvious to everyone. In an imperfect world, it is tested rigorously through changing economic, social, political, environmental, and religious events. Our development of good character is a by-product of our responses, exchanges, and trade-offs within the marketplace. We can never take anyone's practice of "good character" for granted. It is influenced by a lifelong process of discernment with the willingness to confess our mistakes when appropriate and necessary. The temptation, however, is always there to cover up. We are constantly under trial, and our trustworthiness and sustainability can never be taken for granted.

The next chapter emphasizes that our compassion for others can never remain static. Otherwise, we will dampen the organization's spirit, and the public will doubt that we really care. They may also think that our understanding of compassion is incomplete. Leaders who matter demonstrate an underlying wholesomeness and a caring attitude toward everyone's well-being. And the leader's borders of compassion are not limited to one's organization or nation but reach out to the larger human community. The leaders' character as well as compassion are significant qualities in shaping caring organizations with a global outlook.

PART TWO

Ways Organizations Build Community:
Collegiality,
Compassion,
Courage

5
Collegiality

The Pittsburgh Steelers football team is synonymous with the city of Pittsburgh. Some even claim that professional football is the de facto religion of our city. This is how it seemed to many of us when our team went to the Super Bowl in 2006 and 2009 after a long absence from the top. The previous four Steeler championships were won nearly three decades earlier. So going to a second Super Bowl in three years was a big event for Pittsburghers and Steeler fans nationally. I had never seen the city so excited since our family moved to Pittsburgh in 1981. Another piece of information is that my wife, Doris, and our family attend Fox Chapel Presbyterian Church in Pittsburgh, as did coach Bill Cowher of the Steelers and his family until they moved to his wife Kaye's home base in North Carolina. While the Cowhers were with us they became extended family to our church members, with weekend tailgate parties on the church's parking lot when the Steelers were in town. We raised our voices in common cheers for victory.

The Steelers' success owes much to the spirit instilled by the players and coaching staff and backed by the unfailing support of the Rooney family ownership and the wide circle of faithful fans. Put all these factors together, and you will witness a strong spirit of collegiality in action—owners, fans, players, and staff—united as "colleagues" with a common goal, namely, to win the championship as often as possible to bring renewed recognition and fame to Pittsburgh. Besides, it was fun and exciting for us all. The church built community by turning our church

parking lot into a pregame tailgate party on Sundays following our morning church services. Children, friends, and parents had good fellowship,
which is part of an essential collegiality in the life of every organization.

As I reflected on the collective events of Super Bowl week, I realized that collegiality in any form can never be taken for granted. To
tell the truth, we are not always collegial with one another. We have a
tendency to act independently in our daily lives. According to *Webster's
College Dictionary* (Random House), "collegial" implies the "sharing
of responsibility in a group endeavor." It is this common togetherness
that is not seen very often, given the competitiveness and mistrust that
limit our attempts at collegiality. We live in a win/lose culture, and
competition in sports illustrates our preferred cultural lifestyle, namely,
to be a winning team in a winning city. Practicing collegiality in our
organizations is normally what we hope for, but we cannot assume
that it will be present in all areas of our lives, such as business, institutions, homes, and philanthropic endeavors. What can we do, then, to
enhance collegiality among followers, leaders, and supporters interacting with one another?

CONNECT THE DOTS OF OUR COMMON HUMANITY

Robert K. Greenleaf, a former AT&T executive known for his
servant-leadership writings, gave the advice that leadership's first task
is to define reality within the organization, and leadership's final task
is to learn to say "thank you." It sounds simple, but it's often forgotten
within organizational competition and conflict. In between the first and
the last tasks, leadership must assume the role of "servant" and "debtor"
to all the members of the organization as well as the larger community.[1]
Retired CEO Bill George of Medtronics indicates that authentic leadership begins and ends with a genuine expression of appreciation for
everyone's efforts on behalf of the organization.[2] What does this note
of appreciation accomplish? It empowers and connects the dots of our
common humanity. And this common humanity also includes enemies
whom we distrust and even hate at times.

Followers and leaders are defined by the contributions they provide
to the organization and society. If successful, they share values that
improve our lives, services that humanize us, and character traits that
demonstrate honor and respect for one another. Through these means,
initial relationships are built for lasting friendships. In time we will dis-

cover, I believe, that the enduring basis of reality will integrate divine as well as human dimensions if we wish to live and build meaningful lives.

Healthy and trusting relationships are far more enriching than alienation from one another. This is why organizations sensitive to collegiality are careful to respect their retired personnel. Such respect sends a clear message to those currently at work that they, too, will not be forgotten. There is also the message to retirees that collegiality extends throughout the aging process. In our busy and pragmatic lifestyles the enduring significance of collegiality can be easily dismissed as nonessential: we forget that the retirement process within the organization builds an effective core of rooters from the previous generation. Religious institutions that stay in touch with old and young alike understand the importance of this connecting factor; they act responsibly to honor the past while putting in place faithful and promising younger persons for the years ahead. Organizations alert to change are well aware of the ties between past and present personnel.

Peter M. Senge, organizational specialist and faculty member at Massachusetts Institute of Technology (MIT), remarked in honor of Robert Greenleaf's years of service to AT&T that his caring outlook was the core factor behind the building of meaningful relationships in the organizations he counseled. Senge highlighted his comments by saying,

> What have we lost in a "transactional" society, where "What's in it for me?" is the assumed bedrock of all actions? We have lost the joy of "creating," of working for something just because it needs to be done. In our frenzy to get something for ourselves, we have lost ourselves. We have doomed ourselves to a smaller, dull part of life, full of the things we acquire and empty of any deeper happiness. We have forgotten that, as Robert Frost said, "All great things are done for their own sake." To think that this reorientation of spirit might be a foundation for true leadership stunned me.[3]

This confession by Professor Senge ought to be a timely reminder to leaders in all organizations to develop a larger horizon of expectations, never to be self-satisfied with the present nor to limit themselves to a narrow circle of contributors.

Senge also pointed out that we now live in a more dangerous world than a hundred years ago. Why? Because of three primary forces driving our lives today: (1) the emphasis on economic growth, (2) our technological expansion and its future direction, and (3) the growth of global business institutions and the implications of that expansion.

Even though we live longer (seventy-five to eighty years on average), we have more threats and changes now from such things as violence, stress, acid rain, nuclear weapons, drugs, AIDS, the loss of indigenous cultures, and unexpected crashes that occur night and day.[4]

Are there even more crises emerging now than we can handle? It seems that the bedrock of reality today centers on things rather than relationships. What has happened to the fundamental importance of intergenerational relationships fostered in the past by our religious institutions? Senge likewise believes that we have lost the art of dialogue in our business institutions. E-mail and cell phones are not the same as authentic dialogue in person with one another. It is not an either/or matter, but a both/and situation that needs to be balanced in our lives.

I concur with Senge's observation and believe that the art of dialogue may be lost in our religious and nonprofit organizations as well. Aren't we getting more tired than ever from our endless conflicts, regardless of what our social, political, or faith outlooks might be? Perhaps our various institutions have lost the sense of authenticity that once made them so attractive. By not giving one another the space and permission for genuine and honest dialogue, we have largely lost meaningful conversations so necessary to our well-being as an inquiring, learning, and believing community.

Many of today's so-called "dialogues" are superficial discussions to trade repetitive biases with one another. What we need in our organizations, religious and nonreligious, is a place where followers as well as leaders are truly listening and hearing one another. Who is going to do the necessary dialogue modeling that is needed? Bob Galvin, former CEO of Motorola, was quoted as eloquently saying, "My job is to listen to what the organization is trying to say, and then make sure that it gets forcefully articulated."[5] I wonder how many followers need to hear a similar statement from their leaders as well, whatever the nature of the organization might be?

No doubt you have heard the saying in the King James Bible "Where there is no vision, the people perish" (Prov. 29:18). This verse illustrates that the lines of communication between followers and leaders flourish when they have a shared sense of purpose. This is evident when the dots of our common humanity are connected by a common goal. We ought to deepen the level of our dialogues with one another in order to explore the meaning of a shared vision that truly connects us. Reaching this goal is an essential role of effective leadership that is able to articulate persuasively how we might improve our tomorrows together. To aim for such a goal requires that organizations raise serious internal questions such as the following:

—How do shared visions develop?
—How much mutual ownership of our vision is revealed in our conversations together?
—Which of our current shared models need changing?
—How do organizations learn how to learn together?
—Are we ready yet to turn our organizations and institutions into learning (rather than judging) communities in order to claim a shared vision?

Connecting the dots of our common humanity will transform the nobodies silent among us into somebodies willing to do their part to usher us into becoming a community. A community that is excited about its newfound collegiality will build a more meaningful society working together.

AFFIRM ONE ANOTHER'S STRENGTHS

The secret to the success of any organization is how well it affirms and uses the strengths of its members. The process of affirmation and acceptance transforms the organization's lifestyle and vitality. What organization is there that doesn't have room for improvement in fulfilling its mission faithfully and well? This is vital in enabling an organization to communicate effectively its values to customers, clients, and members who believe in its purpose. To serve its community better, any sensitive organization will undertake critical reviews of itself and attempt to learn more about the public's real needs. This collective process of review and evaluation is an ongoing part of learning and change. Being open for change is the key that unlocks the door to every organization's future health and renewed purpose. There is simply no end to change in an enlivened organization that is already adding value and meaning to society and receiving appreciative acknowledgment for its positive role on behalf of the larger community.

To reach a stage of proud respect requires constant experimentation and the willingness to change attitudes on the part of followers and leaders within the organization. Take, for example, the story of a successful family business like Johnsonville Sausage, headed by Ralph Stayer. He learned how to let his workers lead. As he expressed it, "I wanted employees who would fly like geese. What I had was a company that wallowed like a herd of buffalo."[6] It took him ten years to engineer the turnaround, and the process is not over. As he has learned, "change is the real job of every effective business leader because change is about the present and the future, not about the past. There is no end to change."[7] Such a statement could be applied to nonprofit organizations as well.

I have observed in my own leadership roles as a coach and consultant that institutions in all fields require openness to welcome change. The need is not limited to any single class of organizations. For leaders, however, the difficulty with change is how to learn to give up control as leaders in an organization. We need to practice a new paradigm of who is really in charge in the context of change—this becomes more than an issue of governance, which is insufficiently understood today and poorly debated among profit and nonprofit organizations. From my observation of governance issues in organizations, there are usually many parties eager to offer advice but few, if any, willing to assume the burden of responsibility. Let's look at Stayer's revealing story, which points to many of these concerns:

> I hadn't really built the company all alone, but I had created the management style that kept people from assuming responsibility. Of course, it was counter-productive for me to own all the company's problems by myself, but in 1980 every problem did, in fact, rest squarely on my shoulders, weighing me down—though I didn't appreciate it at the time—crippling my subordinates and strangling the company. If I was going to fix what I had made, I would have to start by fixing myself . . . thank God I was the problem so I could be the solution.[8]

As one who has been there and done that, I suspect we could substitute the term "company" for any other organizational name and recognize our own experiences in Stayer's effort to lead change in his family business. Every reader can make his or her own comparison.

As Stayer tells it, he wanted radical change. He envisioned Johnsonville Sausage organizationally becoming like a "flock of geese on the wing." As he expressed it,

> I didn't want an organization chart with traditional lines and boxes, but a "V" of individuals who knew the common goal, took turns leading and adjusted their structure to the task at hand. Geese fly in a wedge, for instance, but land in waves. Most important, each individual bird is responsible for its own performance.[9]

On company organizational charts there is often a gap between the outline and actual practice. Having an organizational outline is not necessarily an answer to our real problems, which is why Stayer's analysis didn't follow an organizational chart. And in reality, how many organizations ignore their chart in effectively conducting their day-to-day practice?

Stayer began his process with an attitude survey of his people—the followers. He discovered that Johnsonville employees scored average marks in commitment to the company, not unlike their counterparts at other big impersonal companies. To put it simply, his employees lacked motivation, and he was startled to discover this. He didn't want to admit that he had a problem. The survey indicated that his people saw nothing for themselves at Johnsonville Sausage. However, he still was unwilling to admit that he was the biggest obstacle to changing their point of view. It became clear with time that if he truly wanted to improve results, he had to increase their involvement and ownership in the business.

Stayer's story goes on to document experiments and improvements over a period of years. On the one hand, he discovered many of the employees unwilling to take on added responsibilities to act like "owners." On the other hand, while he wanted his people to share meaningfully in the decision process, he knew that deep within himself he was in love with his own control. Was he satisfied with just having people guess what he wanted instead of telling them? In his new paradigm, he knew that he hadn't gone far enough in shifting greater responsibility onto the total organization. Many of his people were not yet ready to move with him from point A to point B.

Together they revised their goal from a state of shared responsibility to an environment where people can insist on being responsible. This shift in the paradigm called for him to be more of a player/coach than an authority over his people. Things began to perk up when the followers discovered they had the freedom to increase their output during the week and thereby avoid working on weekends. They reduced their downtime (due to lateness, absences, sloppy maintenance, etc.) and now had Saturdays and Sundays off.

His people continued to gain more confidence in assuming greater responsibility. For instance, customer letters were no longer answered by Stayer but by line workers who made the sausage. The workers also took on most of the traditional personnel functions. They turned themselves from being followers of the organization into becoming

production-performance experts who reviewed performance standards and had the authority to recommend buyouts of people who
were not working up to standards. Previously, organizational longev-
ity had mattered more than performance. This was now changing as
their improvements brought them closer to point B, their target goal
for excellence. In the process, the organization decided to eliminate
the annual across-the-board raise and in its place substituted a pay-for-
responsibility system.

Along with the salary change, the company instituted a "performance
share"—a fixed percentage of pretax profits to be distributed every six
months among employees. Johnsonville Sausage was now sharing profits on the basis of performance, enhancing that "somebody feeling" of
importance within the organization. Do you think nonprofits could
make similar internal changes to create a wider sense of ownership? Is
there a willingness to change in your organization on all levels? Every
organization might wish to discuss that question among themselves.

It is also interesting to note that in Stayer's organization, "the traditional personnel department disappeared and was replaced by a learning
and personnel development team to help individual employees develop
their own Points B and A—their destinations and starting points—and
figure out how to use Johnsonville to reach their goals."[10] This was
followed by establishing an educational allowance for each person, to
be used as the person saw fit. Some took courses in cooking or sewing,
and a few even took flying lessons. Approximately 65 percent of the
employees began to focus on job-related formal learning. Johnsonville
Sausage was truly becoming a learning company that believed in lifelong learning opportunities for its followers and leaders. Stayer was
seeing his vision come alive within the organization—followers had
become leaders, and leaders had become listeners with a player/coach/
consultant model of behavior within the organization. As a company
they have become cooperative stakeholders working together. In this
mutual process of affirmation of one another's strengths everyone has
benefited, and the organization has become more successful. Surely
there are lessons to explore here for nonprofit organizations as well.

According to Stayer, the company's greatest enemy presently is its
success. He feels there has recently been too much self-congratulation
and recognition, which has its hazards. Every organization realizes with
time that nothing is perfect, and when the cause for excitement and
rejoicing is placed in perspective, Johnsonville Sausage isn't really a story
about the importance of change itself but rather about the process used

in producing change—the process of uniting followers and leaders to share a vision but also the significance that sharing learning and responsibilities has for individual workers as well as for organizational fulfillment. Today, Stayer has replaced himself with a new chief operating officer at Johnsonville Sausage. He is now the company's hired consultant.

PROVIDE A CLIMATE OF CONSENSUS

What the Johnsonville Sausage story also highlights is that the pathway to building a climate of consensus is a long and arduous process. In any organization, the process beckons us to be patient. Long-suffering and willingness to forgive one another are essential parts in building relationships. Mistakes will be made, and persons will inevitably feel hurt in the change process. It may seem easier and wiser at times to stick with an authoritative leader operating on yesterday's hierarchical structure. Everyone would then know his or her place, and there would be relative security if the revenue stream remained solid. But as many of us have discovered, nothing is permanent in life or business. For most organizations, change embraced in a spirit of flexibility may in the long run be the wiser path to pursue.

Others might say the best way to judge transitions is to follow whomever you regard as a "great leader," which may involve following him or her out the door. This also has risks if the supply of doors declines in the future. On the other side of the ledger, workers often view "great leaders" as persons who understand that results are achieved not because they have the perfect strategy or know how to give orders, but because they feel empowered to do their very best.[11] In other words, "great leaders" know how to build and maintain a climate of consensus where everyone feels they are being heard and what they contribute counts for something. Outstanding leaders know how to transform followers into leaders with an ear for the changing dynamics of the organization. Walking through the organization regularly and making oneself accessible are also essential to this process of renewal.

To reinforce a climate of consensus with successful results for the organization, we are called to practice the art of genuine forgiveness. This is necessary if we are to maintain healthy relationships and to enjoy honest communication within the company or institution. The practice of honesty also requires us to be willing to practice forgiveness, for we are never as honest as we claim to be. Our understanding of honesty often gets confused with our practice of social etiquette, which tends to slur honesty into "sweet nothings." However, when matters confronting an organization are quite serious, we can't afford sweet nothings. Change, honesty, and the cleansing spirit of forgiveness are more appropriate for organizations seeking improvement, especially if they need to heal emotional wounds and to build teamwork based on trust and openness. Ostensibly healthy relations at the office, plant, or church may not tell the true picture. The reality may be that the organization has been bleeding, broken, and ignored. Leadership ought to express more than an apology to its wounded organization. We need to ask for forgiveness from our people if our apologies are to be successfully heard and the organization's brokenness healed so that an effective turnaround can take place.

Barbara Kellerman, director of the Center for Public Leadership at the John F. Kennedy School of Government at Harvard University, recently wrote an article titled "When Should a Leader Apologize and When Not?" According to Kellerman, "A leader's apology is a performance in which every expression matters and every word becomes part of the public record."[12] A great deal is at stake when a leader apologizes publicly, whether it is to another leader or to a subordinate. Kellerman pragmatically suggests that the refusal to apologize "can be smart or it can be suicidal. Conversely, readiness to apologize can be seen as a sign of strong character or a sign of weakness. A successful apology can turn enmity into personal and organizational triumph—while an apology that is too little, too late, or too transparently tactical can bring on individual and institutional ruin."[13] The remainder of her carefully worded article seeks a thoughtful balance to guide leaders in their discernment between acting or not acting within today's growing "apology culture."

Some of the consequences of not apologizing illustrate many of the abuses that take place within organizations between followers and leaders. Robert W. Fuller, retired president of Oberlin College, wrote a book several years ago titled *Somebodies and Nobodies: Overcoming the Abuse of Rank*.[14] Fuller points to aspects of the pros and cons of today's apology culture. For Fuller the greater underlying factor in our relationships is the matter of "rankism," which he believes is more encompassing than racism, sexism, or ageism in our global society. Fuller speaks to the expectation of greater dignity in a democratic context to make human life more humane and meaningful for each person.

Fuller's emphasis on building a "dignitarian society" addresses the problems of people who feel like "immigrants" lost in the strangeness of a global society. The realities of change make it necessary to improve everyone's communication skills, especially those of recent immigrants. How do we uphold one another's dignity as diversity among us increases? There is also the growing realization that people never completely leave their immigrant beginnings and cultural tastes. Nevertheless, we can still celebrate with pride all new citizenships in a land that provides more opportunity for all families without asking them to forsake their roots.

Building a climate of consensus will become more complex with heightened diversity in organizations. Misunderstandings will occur frequently, and apologies will not convey the same meaning to all parties. Perhaps a deeper understanding of apology as more than a "secular rite of expiation" would lead us to widen our horizon and appreciate new approaches in solving operational problems that have risen in the organization. Greater good can come through wider associations, including caring relationships for one another. To have a collegial spirit within the context of diversity enriches our practice of compassion, the subject of our next chapter.

6

Compassion

One of the unresolved debates on the American scene today centers on issues related to immigration policy. There is no denying that the United States is seen as a nation of opportunity for immigrants. We are proud of our melting-pot history that favors diversity and has been enriched by millions of immigrants for more than four centuries. In recent decades the reasons for their arrival have become more complicated. An estimated 12 million undocumented immigrants now live in the United States, causing a range of concerns for citizens and government officials. Many of the illegal immigrants are from neighboring Mexico and Central America, along with persons from Asia, Africa, Europe, and the Middle East.

In most cases, people from abroad, legal and illegal, have made significant economic contributions as male and female laborers in farming and the food industry, and as workers beautifying our green lawns, landscaping parks and gardens, caring for children, housekeeping and cooking, and assisting in the construction of homes and stores. Persons with Hispanic backgrounds will soon be the largest single minority group in America. Many here are undocumented and would like to become American citizens, but they may not have entered the United States properly through the legal channels of immigration. Although officially regarded as outsiders, they have nevertheless become "insiders" to a degree by giving birth to children in the States or by making positive contributions at work, usually receiving modest wages.

Many undocumented workers are now being apprehended and deported, in many cases straining family bonds and dividing families with young children. Many illegals are willing and able to assume increased debt to pay the legal cost involved with the formal immigration policy, but in the meantime they are being ordered to return to their country of origin. This in turn has triggered the ecumenical rebirth of a new sanctuary movement representing religious institutions whose sacred mission is to be faithful to the theme of Leviticus 19:34, "The alien who resides with you shall be to you as the citizen among you; you shall love the alien as yourself, for you were aliens in the land of Egypt."

These religious institutions have dedicated their sanctuaries as sacred space to practice "prophetic hospitality." While there may be no legal right for churches to act as asylums of safety, United States immigration authorities tend not to raid them to capture undocumented immigrants. No doubt immigration officials remember well the earlier sanctuary movement underway in the 1980s, when congregations during President Reagan's administration risked harboring Central American political refugees in keeping with the church's tradition to set aside space as a sanctuary for those unjustly treated. Leaders and followers in the churches view their actions as acts of compassion in fulfilling the mission of their religious tradition.

Within these religious organizations there is tension and debate over interpretations of their mission in the context of their responsibilities as citizens. Some actively see their religious activism more liberally, while others define their more limited involvement as "compassionate conservatism," with the goal of rewriting current immigration policy through legislation. Actually, there is a growing convergence among liberal and conservative concerns to work for justice and show compassion. In times like these, leadership that matters needs to be engaged in the struggle at all levels of governance. A bottom line for a fair and equitable procedure is required to bring the matter to rest for all interested parties. Building walled borders is not an adequate response in today's changing world. A solution acceptable to all interested parties is necessary for a more stable global society. Otherwise, our current road map will lead to political chaos, causing more harm than good and inhibiting the development of relationships of trust in a fragile world.

In this changing world, no organization is immune from costly conflicts. Wars and uprisings grow from a disregard for the inner dynamics of organizations, tribes, and nations. Taking an innocuous position of organizational neutrality in today's global context of unresolved tensions and troubles is a luxury we can't afford. Tragedies do and will result.

If we take news reports seriously, our global society is suffering terribly on many fronts. And unfortunately there are no easy answers for the hundreds of thousands who are dislocated, disabled, and killed by the present struggles. While we may differ over assigning the blame, millions in the meantime are looking desperately to organizations of all types—profit and nonprofit—for compassionate and generous acts that offer hope where despair and destruction have prevailed.

Leaders and followers who respond with wisdom and imagination to keep human life human can contribute to a meaningful solution. While we know there are no perfect answers, good ideas will surface among leaders and followers practicing faith, goodwill, and perseverance. This can open pathways of tangible hope to initiate creative beginnings for all concerned. The politics of compassion is actually an unfolding reality seen in bits and pieces; our relationships are slowly mending through a forgiving spirit that draws the brokenhearted together for mutual support. Caring and compassionate leadership can foster positive change. Only then can we begin to approach meaningfully the unanswered question "How in the world can we live together?"

Naturally, we would like to achieve success in these relationships more quickly. But unfortunately the peace process, leading to a constructive resolution of our differences, takes time. This is why the journey is so stressful and why progress is inevitably slow. The mountains of mistrust, the tragic loss of lives, and the persistent memories of survivors all stand in the way of renewed relationships. It seems that those who hate together stick together wherever conflict is exacerbated across racial, ethnic, economic, religious, or political lines. The result has been costly for millions in need. Unresolved power conflicts are still ruling the day in many corners of our world. Worthy organizations large and small are struggling to help people in need, especially those unable to free themselves from harsh realities.

Where then is the hope for those in need? Do we simply accept the fact that the abused will always be with us? Isn't that what the pious have repeated through the years? Do we think we can ever live in a world without poverty and illness? It would be nice, but is it realistic? How many Mother Teresas, Gandhis, and Martin Luther Kings are there today willing to demonstrate their compassion and even die to alleviate ills of whatever nature? We seem to lack able candidates who can step up to bear the burdens of humankind, preoccupied as many are in defending national interests, pursuing personal ambitions, or fulfilling family wishes. How do we respond to a needy global society? Generous donations to worthy causes won't be enough. What's actually required are international leadership talents. More than ever, younger leaders must step in for the aging faithful, spark new energy and ideas, invest in innovative projects, and explore the challenges globally and universally in space.

APPLY THE ESSENCE OF THE GOLDEN RULE

As a consequence, a new wave of leaders are now being educated in the politics of compassion and the skills of social entrepreneurship (doing well while doing good) for the needs of today's and tomorrow's global society. Innovative centers of support are emerging to transcend the status quo of the world's poor, but unfortunately not yet in sufficient number. We are in the early stages of educating future social entre-preneurs to be self-supporting and to teach others to do likewise. This process of instruction is taking place in a growing number of today's forward-looking business schools to enhance the quality of life of millions of persons in poverty. These "social enterprisers," with their self-generated earnings, are building new social networks of the like-minded through Twitter and Facebook to market ideas and cooperate together to raise the standard of life wherever grassroots poverty exists.

I was first introduced to the idea of social entrepreneurship when I was invited to Oxford University as a Senior Academic Fellow at Harris Manchester College. On the Oxford campus, I was introduced to the Said Graduate School of Business and its Skoll Center for Social Entrepreneurship. Oxford University consists of thirty-nine colleges and graduate programs, each with its own community of talented faculty. These learning institutions wisely permit many crossover experiences for students and guests that we found stimulating during our stay at Oxford in the spring of 2006. I particularly valued my contacts with the Said faculty, students, and administrative staff. I'm also grateful for the insights gained from attending classes and meeting with guest scholars and business leaders visiting the Said Business School. An innovative and welcoming spirit was evident at the college.

When we returned home to Pittsburgh, I learned that social entrepreneurship courses had also been introduced at many American graduate schools of business, as well as related academic programs in urban affairs and international relations. In an important sense, I discovered social entrepreneurship to be an application of the Golden Rule for a business-oriented world. Emerging social entrepreneurs are being taught to empower the poor to help themselves and their communities to succeed. The essence of the Golden Rule, in its many indigenous expressions, is basically this underlying sense of respectful care for our common humanity. Here is a small sampling of its expression from a variety of traditions and outlooks around the world.[1]

Do to others as you would have them do to you.

(Luke 6:31)

What you do not want done to yourself, do not do to others.

(Confucius's saying)

"Just as you did it to one of the least of these . . . you did it to me."
(Matt. 25:40)

We should behave to our friends as we would wish our friends to behave to us.

(Aristotle, *Nicomachean Ethics*)

Act only on that maxim through which you can at the same time work for that it should become a universal law.

(Immanuel Kant, *Groundwork of the Metaphysics of Morals*)

Treat with kindness your parents and kindred, and orphans and those in need. Speak fair to the people; be steadfast in prayer; and practice regular charity.

(Qur'an 2:83)

Behind this range of expressions related to the Golden Rule is a single underlying assumption: namely, that everyone is entitled to the same dignity and respect we desire for ourselves. From my perspective, the theological rationale that upholds humankind is the belief that we are created in God's image, implying that the sacred respect offered to

God is to be extended toward everyone else created in the divine image. Herein lies the essence of the Golden Rule—it serves as an ethical measurement for that respectful quality of relationships we ought to practice with one another. Unfortunately, we tend to live among broken relationships, fueled by endless conflicts and suspicions that undermine trust among us. If we were to receive a report card on our practice of the Golden Rule, I suspect most of us might not score as high as we would like; likewise, fewer of us are really as low as we think we are.

I have long felt that God has many surprises (some even shocking) in store for us. We would be much better off if we weren't in the business of second-guessing with God. In our effort to be realistic, we ought instead to confess that we all tend to rationalize about our actual behavior as we stray from the standards of the Golden Rule not only in our organizational life but also in our personal dealings with one another.

CEO Max DePree of Herman Miller, Inc., the furniture maker, has written a number of books on leadership.[2] He emphasizes that organizations that excel are communities that practice human respect based on the spirit of the Golden Rule. Such respect is evident in a number of ways, such as the compensation scale at Herman Miller where teamwork is the motto. Nationwide, there is an increasing gap between followers and leaders in their earnings—currently the CEO's earnings in the United States on average, with added stock options, are five hundred times the hourly worker's wage. This leads us to question if the spirit of the Golden Rule is truly being followed. As DePree has said, "When leaders indulge themselves with lavish perks and the trappings of power, they are damaging their standing as leaders."[3]

The compensation scale actually assigns monetary values to the intrinsic worth of persons within the organization, especially between management and followers who like to believe they are working as a team to advance the organization's mission. As a team, the values and character of both followers and leaders ought to uphold a common willingness to support a sense of fairness as understood by all parties. As CEO Bill George, author of *Authentic Leadership: Rediscovering the Secrets to Creating Lasting Value*, expresses it, "When employees believe their work has a deeper purpose, their results will vastly exceed those who use only their minds and bodies. This will become the company's competitive advantage."[4] To foster teamwork, a commitment to fairness (not sameness) should be expressed through fair compensation and recognition throughout the organization.

When the spirit of the Golden Rule is upheld, the quality of inter-relationships within the organization is raised and a caring quality of compassion becomes the underlying adhesive that bonds individuals together. In fact, it can be said that compassion is embedded in the Golden Rule, unifying followers and leaders as fellow somebodies with dignity in the organization. This spirit will be conveyed to others throughout the community. Such an outlook will erase or at least greatly diminish the feeling of "rankism" within the organization. Perhaps the poet Robert Browning had it right when he wrote,

> All service ranks the same with God:
> With God whose puppets, best and worst,
> are we; there is no last nor first.[5]

The American playwright Tennessee Williams also expresses a similar concern from his experience:[6] The public somebody you are when you have a "name" is a fiction. The only somebody worth being is the solitary and unseen you that existed from your first breath and is the sum of your actions. This unseen you is constantly in a state of becoming under your own volition—and knowing those things, you can even survive, notes Williams, the catastrophe of success.

The Golden Rule reminds us then that everyone is somebody. There are no nobodies unless you allow someone's remarks for good or ill to dictate your lifestyle and reactions. I can remember early in life a recurring dialogue within myself to place in perspective those unkind "barbs" that were addressed to me. In my private meditations, I would review shortcomings that I was aware of and pray for their correction, including my own negative attitudes toward my critics. An important part of anyone's prayer life is this struggle to practice authentic humility. Prayer also helps to nurture the creative flow in us, overcoming that "play-it-safe" mind-set that can also be a detriment to the organization, especially when we are tempted to submit to the political dictates of the moment. If you too have had any of these feelings, you can understand the negative dynamics at work preventing the organization from moving forward.

For a time, I blamed my shortcomings on my immigrant Armenian parents and their unfamiliarity with American culture, which was so apparent living in our neighborhood in Los Angeles. Although I was born in the United States, my parents had married in the Middle East and later left their limited freedom at a time when many fellow Armenians were also suffering from their minority status as Christians. My father, uneducated in American ways, worked hard in his small business and had only modest results. He died when I was thirteen; my sister and I were raised by my mother, who started her own dressmaking shop from home. She later felt the need for greater social contact in the city and took a job with other women as a seamstress in a unionized factory.

My mother's coworkers came from many national backgrounds, exposing our family to an even greater multicultural outlook on life. I was raised in a household where four languages were heard—Armenian, Turkish, Arabic, and English. I started elementary school stuttering; it wasn't long before the kindergarten teacher encouraged my parents to allow me to speak English at home; then the stuttering left. Later, as I was pursuing doctoral studies in German at the University of Basel in Switzerland, I learned more fully what a rich and varied cultural history I had inherited from my parents. I was more proud than ever of their struggles and accomplishments in spite of their English deficiency, and I regretted my early youthful judgments of their shortcomings.

It was my mother's savvy ability to survive that taught my sister and me not to be ashamed of our modest lifestyle or the struggles with language and culture encountered by my parents in their social contacts. I was glad for their keen passion to see that we were well educated, which in turn deepened my respect for the American Armenian heritage I received from them.

What my mother didn't understand when I was an undergraduate student at Occidental College was my growing sense of a call to be a parish pastor. What a waste, my mother thought! "You can be a good Christian," she said, "and become a businessman or a lawyer." Her feeling was quite similar to many practical immigrants who wish to succeed in a world of dollars and cents. She would add, "Here you are, born in America," she said, "with all the opportunities for education and advancement, but why pastoral ministry?" She died of cancer at the age of fifty-one, the day after I passed the ordination exams that qualified me for a church position. I was grateful that God had kept my mother alive to see me anticipate my ministry and to give me her blessing.

I share this story because my parents not only loved us but taught us the lesson of the Golden Rule—namely, to practice compassionate respect toward others as the common ground for keeping human life human before God, in whose image we are all created. My mother suffered as a young woman, like so many Armenians of her generation, yet she did not lose her perspective on the importance of human dignity and respect for all people, including one's enemies (Luke 6:35).

EXERCISE YOUR GENEROSITY OF SPIRIT

With compassion as the core message of the Golden Rule, we are also expected to practice a generous spirit in our relationships with one another. This spirit of generosity has a positive impact on advancing ethical conduct within our organizations and communities. If we find it difficult to express generosity at home or in the organizations we serve, we will find it even harder to be generous to strangers, let alone our enemies. Yet this is the standard expected of us if we claim to be compassionate followers and leaders. When we are candid with ourselves, our practice of compassion in our associations with others is less than sterling. We tend to watch our manners and do what is expected when convenient; but frankly, for the most part, we pay attention to personal interests and family concerns first. There is only so much time in a day, we rationalize with ourselves. Being compassionately ethical, however, is much more than the practice of social etiquette and modest acts of charity toward others in need.

In my research on marketplace ethics, I sent surveys (designed with the assistance of experienced persons in data gathering) to business and professional leaders to register their ethical attitudes and practices in the marketplace. We invited those who received the survey to respond anonymously. (See the appendix, pp. 112–16, for a copy of the Marketplace Ethics Questionnaire.) Over 20 percent of those receiving the survey responded, and approximately half of the respondents, by their choice, included a signed letter along with a copy of the ethical code of conduct adopted by their organization.

Here is one of the survey questions asked: "How do you understand the phrase 'business is business'?" Their responses could be one of the following: _____ anything goes; _____ money talks; _____ don't expect generosity; _____ everyone has a price; _____ other. The vast majority of participants indicated that the phrase "business is business" is associated in their minds with the phrase "don't expect generosity." In other words, the usual outlook for financially oriented participants in all types of organizations, regardless of what they say publicly, is to expect payment (or gifts) for their services if they are to pay their employees and support their volunteers. If "business is business," in other words, it means we can't expect generosity and at the same time function adequately in the marketplace. Is this what we expected to find? Are you surprised and perhaps even shocked with the prevailing response from participants in the survey?

Frankly, there are differences between what we believe is the right thing to do and what our profession obligates us to do. For instance, we know there are helping professionals (doctors, lawyers, clergy, etc.) who would like to follow their consciences and provide professional services without necessarily expecting compensation. Haven't we all felt the urge to act generously at times? Perhaps this may explain in part why the public is confused or even angry when our own professional organizations insist that pay standards be upheld before service is rendered. When money becomes the issue that tests the quality of our relationships, the realization becomes clearer that we live in an economically driven culture where "business is business." Public disappointment then mounts in our exchanges with one another, and we feel either guilty or self-righteous under pressure to defend our respective positions. We ought to "keep our cool," but, honestly, it is sometimes too difficult, especially in health, legal, and educational concerns.

At the same time, almost 90 percent of the respondents to our survey claimed a religious affiliation, whether Protestant, Catholic, Orthodox, Jewish, Muslim, Hindu, or other. I mention this to say that major religious traditions do emphasize the importance of having a generous spirit but in reality advise cautious financial guidelines. We need to be aware of the gap between the teachings of our faith traditions and actual practice. This may explain in part the disappointment many nonprofit organizations encounter when potential donors fail to respond to fundraising efforts. Some donors may lack an adequate understanding of the organization's relevance, but whatever the case, there is far less generosity of spirit within communities than many organizations are willing to admit. It may take a sudden crisis to make us aware of how little we have been doing, in spite of our rhetoric to the contrary. Generosity of spirit is actually an expression of our ethical conduct, and when this is clearly understood, more of us might be willing to lift one another to a higher level of accountability. What's needed is a more inclusive spirit of compassion as an expression of our ethical conduct in deeds that will benefit today's global society.

In reality, we are as ethical in our practices as the last time we made a serious appraisal of our organizational giving before the larger community. What organization has not been tempted to reduce its ethical obligations and public services during tough times, rationalizing that they must first take care of "their own," but thereby limiting their sphere of action to their own people within the global village?

As I reflected on these personal and public shortcomings, I was inspired to set forth my own personal "ten commandments" as guidelines for the marketplace that would apply to us all in our common humanity.

Ten Strategic Guidelines for the Marketplace

We are all as ethical as the last time we were tempted. None of us is immune; we are tested daily as we act according to self-interest, priorities, and values. Admitting mistakes is the first step to restoring broken relationships and reputation.

It is not easy to sort out what is and what is not negotiable for us in a market-driven society with its tempting and questionable trade-offs. To enable us to trade upward rather than downward, the following guidelines provide a framework within which to examine our fears, failures, rationalizations, and excuses.

1. Regard individuals as persons who are more than a means to another's end. To manipulate one another defaces the humanity that resides in us.
2. Be generous. The benefits will exceed the cost in the long term. The propensity for greed actually depersonalizes us, whereas the practice of generosity has the power to reconnect us with our humanity. Healthy relationships are linked to generosity that fosters efficiency in our dealings with one another.
3. Practice moderation. Obsession with winning often leads to cheating and is destructive. Competition is inevitable, but why waste ourselves in seeking to win at any cost? The outcome is generally a lose-lose proposition for everyone. This is why rules and regulations become necessary to foster fair competition and to come to terms with our human nature, whatever its imperfect tendencies.
4. Disclose mistakes. Admitting error and making restitution are necessary means to restoring moral character. Being ethical is never cheap, but succumbing to temptation can be even more damaging.
5. Arrange priorities. Set long-range goals, and keep principles in mind. In the midst of marketplace trade-offs, distinguishing between primary and secondary priorities becomes an imperative. Priorities that honor life are primary and nonnegotiable.

6. Keep promises. Trust, confidence, and authenticity are built over time. There is no easy formula for building trust; it needs to be earned daily.

7. Tell the truth. Falsifying information destroys credibility. Lying is endemic to our lives; even etiquette sometimes fosters lying, destroying candor in our relationships. Speaking the truth is not a science; it is an art fortified by caring concern for others.

8. Exercise a more inclusive sense of giving. Charity begins locally but needs to extend far beyond our homes and neighborhoods.

9. Insist on being well informed. Judgment without adequate knowledge is fatal. We can't afford to be driven by rumor rather than facts. Having all the facts may be impossible, but we must nevertheless maximize our knowledge as a prerequisite for wiser decisions.

10. Be productive without losing yourself in the process. Evaluate your life in light of your trade-offs—the meaning of success is much more than an accounting of dollars and cents. Nurture a life outside of work, work, work for a whole and healthy life.

Translating these ten guidelines into our lives and into codes of ethics for organizations and company policies will support the health of the marketplace as we evaluate daily trade-offs. We may only be able to approximate these strategic guidelines, but in so doing we will raise the ethical level of business, show respect to others, experience personal growth, encourage efficiency, heighten listening, and increase productivity—all characteristics of successful companies and organizations seeking a sustainable and fulfilling future. Being ethical in the marketplace is simply doing what's right with a sense of compassion and regard for one another. We thereby honor the divine image in everyone we encounter, no matter how defaced the enemy may appear.

PRACTICE DIGNITY WITHOUT DEPENDENCE

Our respect for human dignity grows when we practice compassion without strings attached, expecting no obligation from the people we serve. Anticipating a payoff or reward for doing good and being compassionate actually negates whatever kindness we have shown. It is unfortunate when followers and leaders expect something in return.

This is how Lao Tzu wisely cautioned us from the viewpoint of his Eastern tradition:[7]

> The best of all leaders is the one who helps people so that, eventually, they don't need him. . . .
>   Then comes the one they love and admire.
>   Then comes the one they fear.
>   The worst is the one who lets people push him around.
>   Where there is no trust, people will act in bad faith.
>   The best leader doesn't say much, but what he says carries weight.
>   When he is finished with his work, the people say, "It happened naturally."

Unhealthy dependence does not enable followers to develop. In the midst of our strength, we must remind ourselves that we are also weak. If we have the need to be dependent—and I suspect we all feel the need at times—such dependence should be first lodged in the depth of our faith and candor. For me, authentic dependence is centered in faithfulness as expressed in Proverbs 3:5–6:

> Trust in the LORD with all your heart,
>   and do not rely on your own insight.
> In all your ways acknowledge him,
>   and he will make straight your paths.

Healthy dependence in practice is found in this divine relationship if we are willing to maintain and deepen it on a regular basis in our times of quiet and honest prayer. In reality, we find that we can't equate our faithfulness with the unfailing divine faithfulness that supports us. Broken promises, unfortunately, characterize human history before God and with one another. The psalmist in Scripture understood well our faulty human nature as expressed in Psalm 139:1: "O LORD, you have searched me and known me. . . ."

That's why the practice of forgiveness is so essential in maintaining relationships—divine and human—alive and healthy, enabling us to be trustworthy as we develop our maturity in sync with one another. In organizational life, saying no is as important as saying yes in our team development and is in keeping with our dignity. None of us has a monopoly on understanding the mystery of maturity in ourselves and its benefits in fulfilling the organization's mission. In this growth process, we are called to be generous and supportive within the limits of our wisdom, knowing that there will be times to ask forgiveness when promises are unmet and when we struggle to understand why.

Dignity without dependence is the wisest way to build a team spirit of interdependence within an organization and institution. This is an important way to maintain trust and fulfill the organization's mission. Leadership guru John W. Gardner added this sage piece of advice:[8]

> Leaders must understand that for men and women the driving energies are latent. Some individuals are unaware of their potentialities; some are sleepwalking through the routines of life; some have succumbed to a sense of defeat. What leaders see on the surface can be discouraging—people, even very able people, caught in the routines of life, thinking short-term, placing narrow self-beneficial furrows through life. What leaders have to remember is that somewhere under that somnambulant surface is the creature that builds civilizations, the dreamer of dreams, the risk taker. And, remembering that, the leader must reach down to the springs that never dry up, the ever fresh springs of the human spirit.

From an international perspective, Jean Monnet of France and Mahatma Gandhi of India both practiced dignity without dependence while seeking to lead in their unique ways. Monnet envisioned a unified Europe after World War II, and Gandhi wanted India to have the self-respect to be a sovereign nation, no longer a colony of England. Both were seeking dignity and a greater freedom for their regions. Both had the naiveté, vision, and faith of young people. Monnet knew in one sense that all the combatants would leave catastrophes behind them, and a vision to unite a war-torn Europe was of paramount concern to him. Gandhi wanted to free his people from a dehumanizing dependence on England that was denying them freedom and dignity. Each showed great determination and humility to reach the goal although each man approached the challenge differently.

Gandhi initiated a peaceful, nonviolent resistance known as satyagraha, while Monnet used a self-denying spirit of persuasion with major world leaders. Monnet understood the egos and needs of these leaders and was able to influence them without being in the forefront himself. He ceded the headlines to others as he worked quietly and persuasively behind the scenes. Howard Gardner, in his book *Leading Minds: An Anatomy of Leadership*,[9] describes how Monnet and Gandhi modeled dignity without dependence on the pressures faced in each of their respective circles. Gardner also inspired me to reflect on the earlier roles of George Washington as our first president and Abraham Lincoln as our leader through the terrible and painful Civil War. Each sought to establish dignity without an unhealthy dependence on himself, encouraging us to focus our faith in God and the rightness of the future course of our nation to be free, fruitful, and united.

As we consider the compassionate leaders mentioned in our discussion, I find myself wondering, "What were the key questions these leaders asked before they took action and made their commitment?" Peter Drucker sets forth a list of eight questions that might have been considered in one form or another by leaders in every era and in changing situations.[10] First, what needs to be done if compassion for people and dignity are to be realized? The focus before leading must be clear and single-minded. Second, what is the right thing to do to fulfill one's mission and destiny in life? The right thing needs to engage all the stakeholders in the enterprise—whether leading a country or building an organization. Third, everyone who leads needs to develop an action plan that can be followed; the plan should also be flexible enough for unexpected outcomes.

Fourth, leaders must take responsibility for their decisions. This sense of responsibility belongs to the entire team of followers and leaders who are accountable for executing the decisions. In the process, changes in leadership roles might be required and should not be delayed. To tolerate nonperforming people in important jobs is demoralizing for the enterprise.

Fifth, the team needs to take responsibility for communicating information about the progress or lack of it to all the followers and leaders on the home front. We need to keep in mind that organizations "are held together by information rather than by ownership or command."[11] Having good information is essential in fulfilling the organization's mission.

Sixth, leadership must focus on opportunities rather than problems. Working on opportunities and having results will lift the spirit of the country or organization. At one point as president of Pittsburgh Seminary, I recall saying to colleagues that I no longer wanted to dwell on the "war stories" that belonged to the school's past, and I hoped that trustees, colleagues, and staff would join me in this practice. I wanted to invest our energy toward the opportunities before us—otherwise we would miss those goals by endlessly dwelling on past stories that reinforced certain debilitating biases.

Seventh, team and community meetings need to be well attended and organized to be productive. Gatherings should be work sessions ready to make decisions rather than engage in repetitious talk. To work ahead and review the agenda of a forthcoming meeting will make discussion and meeting more fruitful.

Eighth and last, leaders need to develop the conscious feeling throughout the organization that everyone is part of a "we" team, not an "I" team. Leaders shouldn't think or say "I" but rather "we." Effective executives know that they have ultimate responsibility, which can "be neither shared nor delegated. But they have full authority only because they have the trust of the organization."[12] This level of trust, we must confess, is difficult to achieve consistently, but I have no doubt Drucker is right to emphasize it if we truly wish to be a productive team that is compassionate and respectful of individual dignity throughout the organization and is able to express its values to the larger community as well. Our final chapter turns our attention to the inevitable task of facing tough changes with courage.

7

Courage

Asma Jahangir, a Pakistani lawyer, is one of the most courageous leaders of human rights issues today. Her name first came to my attention in 1994 when my wife, Doris, and I visited Pakistan to lecture at a graduate theological school located near Lahore, where Jahangir was born in 1952 to an upper-class Muslim family.

Jahangir is proud of her Muslim identity but is saddened by the current religious conflicts and misunderstandings in the world. She claims that "Islam is no more violent or neutral than any other religion in the world—it is just that many Muslim countries have politicized religion for the benefit of the rulers. There are Christian fanatics and Hindu fanatics too—put a gun in the hands of any of them and they terrorize people."[1]

At the time of our visit to Pakistan, Jahangir was engaged in a high-profile case representing two Christians—a father and his fourteen-year-old son. The case was receiving a great deal of discussion, both on the seminary campus where I was lecturing and among members of the Christian minority throughout the country. The two had been sentenced to death by the Lower Court after being found guilty of blasphemy for defacing the Qur'an in their village. Both maintained their innocence and were convinced that they had been framed by another villager who had an interest in their property. The two had appealed the verdict to the Higher Court. Jahangir, also a Muslim, offered to defend the case as a civil rights issue on behalf of the two Christians before the High Court, against the advice of fellow Muslims. Needless to say, her part in the case did not endear her to Islamic authorities governed by their divine law, the Shariah.

STEP UP AND BE ACCOUNTABLE

As it turned out, Asma Jahangir had the courage of her conviction that the two accused Christians had the right of appeal before the High Court. She also worried about her own safety, and subsequently two attempts were made on her life.

Doris and I remember well one evening when we were having dinner at the home of our host, the principal of the theological school. Our meal was interrupted when a seminary staff informed us that the High Court had acquitted the father and son and overturned the Lower Court's earlier decision. With hope against hope that this would be the outcome, their supporters had arranged for the two to leave almost immediately for the airport. An unnamed European country had offered to provide the two with emergency asylum.

In the meantime, the principal of the theological school had quickly informed students, faculty, and staff to remain on campus as a cautionary step. He was fearful that the High Court decision would trigger a dangerous situation. Jahangir's legal stature to uphold the country's civil rights stood out as an important witness that informed citizens and observers alike that courageous public leadership still matters when it enhances the quality of life of all its people.

Many in Pakistan and elsewhere aware of Asma Jahangir's courageous example on behalf of human dignity see her as someone to emulate. She continues today to be deeply involved through the Human Rights Commission of Pakistan, which she helped to establish in 1986.

Courageous leadership is found whenever we respond with candor to what needs to be confronted, although honesty is not necessarily what everyone wishes to hear. Such moments are catalytic in transforming followers into leaders and leaders into listeners who can hear clearly a message requiring top priority in order to advance the institution's mission. The courageous leader must uphold a progressive grasp of reality that enables the organization to overcome its fears and realize its goal. An expression of courage in word and deed enables us to act effectively in exercising leadership and not submit to outside control or be manipulated by false promises.

Only a leader with a courageous spirit and the right cause can step up in an authoritarian climate to move others with the power of his or her own conviction. If the message is persuasive, it becomes a shared idea to transform both the community and the organization into dynamic teams to improve the situation. Even in times of serious crisis, leadership that demonstrates faith and courage provides authentic and exemplary service to others. The leader's public accountability is then more readily accepted by fellow members within the organization as well as by the surrounding community.

KNOW THAT LEADERSHIP IS LONELY

However, there are also times when the process of persuasion fails and the crisis is brought to the chief's door for quick action. Such times are lonely moments for leaders—such as those experienced by Abraham Lincoln in the Civil War, by Lyndon Johnson during the Vietnam conflict, and more recently by George W. Bush and Barack Obama in the current Iraq and Afghanistan struggles, which have lasted even longer than the others. Every president has advisors for a range of political considerations to help interpret events, but no one can expect to resolve these issues without paying a much higher price than imagined in loss of lives and limbs among citizens and combatants.

If we have learned anything from our nation's history, we know that past, present, and future events are interrelated. For instance, present unrest has roots in past decisions, and today's battles have a bearing on whatever emerges tomorrow in the shape of peace or renewed conflict. All decisions have past, present, and future consequences. Followers and leaders, whatever their age and outlook, need to be in sync. Past and present lessons of history need to be studied anew by young and old alike. This calls for critical and constructive listening to one another's interpretation of history before we draw whatever "conclusions" are likely to yield a clearer path; we need to remain mindful of our constricting biases, which need to be shared openly and reevaluated.

Wise people caught in unfortunate battles must explore new directions with humility and dispatch. In the final analysis, to prolong our errors is wrong. Can we ever be sure we have interpreted and followed the divine will as correctly as we had intended? I believe Lincoln was wrestling with similar questions in his "Meditation on the Divine Will" (September 3, 1862; see the appendix, p. 104, for a copy of Lincoln's prayerful reflection as the president seeks a meaningful conclusion to America's costly Civil War). Many scholars of the period believe it to be his greatest speech as president of the United States. The contents are useful for our reflection, as every generation seeks to determine which side of any battle rightfully upholds God's interest. Read the text for yourself the next time you are confronting a major conflict or seeking direction for yourself. Professor Ronald A. Heifetz of Harvard University, a specialist in psychiatry and organizational behavior, was insightful to entitle his helpful book *Leadership without Easy Answers.*[2] Heifetz has a realistic grasp of Lincoln's situation, faced as the president was by a war-time cabinet of critics with wounded memories and grieving families in a divided nation. Winning and losing are never without costs for all parties involved in the battle. Lincoln could not escape this reality. At the same time, he wanted to stay faithful to his war message to keep the country united.

On a much reduced scale from Lincoln, I too have found my leadership challenges to be intellectually demanding. I was driven to advance the seminary's task of theological education by assisting the churches and its institutions to think critically and constructively on the ways and means to renew the mission of reconciliation in a changing world. Producing seminary graduates as leaders for scattered communities is difficult enough, but, without easy solutions, adding on the burdens of society makes the situation more complex than ever. In fact, many outsiders saw our mission as either impossible or irrelevant. Besides, everyone had too many troubles of his or her own to really worry about seminaries. Instead, some folks would naively ask me, "Do you enjoy being president of the seminary?" I usually found myself saying, "Eighty percent of the time; there's a difficult 20 percent that I could live without if I had a choice to do so." Privately, I found myself suspicious of anyone who says he or she loves being a leader of any organization all the time, not willing to admit publicly at least the number of frustrations and disappointments that exist without solutions, knowing that most responses may be fruitless.

The realities of our lives are filled with ambiguities, and this is certainly true in our organizational life. This is why followers and leaders, faced with demanding and unhappy decisions, ought to have their own private spaces as sanctuaries for emotional rest and reflection. Quiet moments of disciplined meditation offer one a chance to review issues that may have been neglected or handled foolishly. In a more prayerful context, we can confess our doubts and anxieties, thereby strengthening our inner soul, where the heart of leadership resides and listens for divine guidance.

During the heat of the American Civil War, Abraham Lincoln often shared his reflective insights and attitudes (including his humor) through brief and brilliant addresses to the citizenry. He warned against being too judgmental at the end of the war, or else we would neglect our prophetic mandate to provide justice with mercy to unify our nation. Lincoln, like Martin Luther King Jr. during the height of our civil rights struggles, was aware of his unpopularity in many sections of the country due to his marches and the battles still to be fought.

Lincoln realized every day that he lived in harm's way, but he nevertheless continued his course of action to reunite the United States, even if it would cost him, as it did King a century later, his life. Fear as well as the reality of being despised can restrict our commitment to do the right thing in fulfilling our responsibilities. As a result, we can leave a trail of broken promises to our core values.

People of faith in almost every religious tradition are instructed to "fear not," but we nevertheless continue to persist in our fears, keeping silent in the face of possible threats. Many persons may sympathize with our dilemmas, but they too remain quiet. Looking back on American history, I have wondered how many of us would have laid aside our doubts to volunteer to join George Washington's patriots in 1776 against the superior and feared British army. We have been educated and conditioned since birth to exercise common sense and not to make foolish decisions. The rebels of 1776 might be seen with hindsight as acting with an uncommon-sense conviction that saw the rebellion as the right and just thing to do.

The political situation was even worse for Lincoln—in his time it was Americans vs. Americans—"right" vs. "right," if you will. This is one of the worst possible conditions for any leader or follower to digest. Lincoln knew that his decision would surely lead to bloodshed and severed relationships between North and South. Such are also the current tragedies and fragmented conditions now prevailing in the Middle East and elsewhere in our conflicted world.

Americans, like others around the world, are anxious about their welfare in light of today's serious recession. Many question the future status of the United States as a superpower. No doubt the complex picture of global power is already expanding and changing. Many of us can recall the story of Goliath in the Bible (1 Samuel 17), who was slain by the smooth stones thrown by a modest shepherd boy named

David. The story ought to cause us to stop and rethink our understanding of "homeland security" today. Are we so wary of strangers on our streets or on planes that we are becoming paranoid? The fear of terrorism has put us on the defensive regarding our relationships in a global society, especially toward strangers whose skin color and accent may be different from ours. In the present climate of mistrust, how long can we maintain significant international student exchange programs and world trade relations? Where has our courage gone? Is the dust of 9/11 still controlling the psyche of world traders, working harder than ever to make as much money as they can as long as they can? No doubt these thoughts have crossed your minds as they have mine.

Renowned Catholic theologian Thomas Aquinas long ago defined courage as "firmness of spirit in the face of adversity." Aquinas was aware that times like ours call for active and passive courage at the same time. Active courage is our capacity to address and attack problems now, not to pretend they don't exist or to live behind a mask of false optimism. Passive courage, on the other hand, is the endurance on our part to stay in touch in a digital age and to show resilience in knowing that we are all somebodies who have no wish to become nobodies in an alarmist context. The soul of an organization is reinforced in such times by thoughtful leaders and followers who show the courage, creativity, and compassion to reach out and take the needed risk to open new lines of communication with strangers and even enemies. Are we not all in need of developing global neighborhoods? There we can connect with one another's humanity and solidify common ground and common yearnings from one another's understanding of faith, hope, and love. Is having such an expectation only an impossible dream, a fading myth no longer possible? For your sake and mine, I hope not. The remaining hope we share needs to be translated into positive deeds if the spirit of the rainbow is to be visible within everyone's horizon.

ADDRESS DISAPPOINTMENT
WITH UNCOMMON WISDOM

God has not abandoned us to despair. Building castles on the beach is fun with children and grandchildren, but in itself it is not enough to prepare them for a changing world. Nor do I believe that any static religion, business, government, or professional practice that is not undergoing a learning process of growth can keep us from having restless feelings.

Opportunities that surface in every age throughout human history are challenges to the existing status quo. Another way of envisioning this is to realize that we are truly born to be reformers, to hike to the highest mountaintop near us to see beyond our disappointments, and in the process to be humbled by the rainbow that appears after the storm, with its possibilities of hope.

Disappointments can also be overcome when we view life as an endless adventure in practicing divinely inspired, uncommon wisdom that unites heaven and earth when we succeed, drawing us closer to the rainbow of hope in all its splendor. But without the toughness of heart, mind, and soul working together, we will be unable to reach the levels of creativity and energy lying dormant within us. We will miss the divine destiny envisioned for us unless we exercise wise stewardship of our endowed talents, accepting our responsibility to care for this universe invested in us since the beginning of time.[3]

Human leadership is blessed, I believe, with a toughness of spirit witnessed already in dedicated lives past and present. Take the story of Sir Ernest Shackleton, the sea captain who led the celebrated British polar expedition to the coast of Antarctica. His ship the *Endurance* sailed from England in 1914 on the brink of World War I. Shackleton made the first public announcement of the expedition in an advertisement for volunteers: "Men wanted for Hazardous Journey, small wages, bitter cold, long months of complete darkness, constant danger, safe return doubtful. Honor and recognition in case of success."[4] He received five thousand applicants for his small crew of twenty-seven. He divided his candidates into three categories—"Mad," "Hopeless," and "Possible."

Shackleton limited his interview process to the "Possible" category by relying on his instinct for judging character. He essentially omitted the categories of "Mad" and "Hopeless." He sought individuals who expressed realistic optimism, cheerfulness with a sense of humor, competence in the requisite skills, and above all a demonstrated record of perseverance. His reasoning became clear when the *Endurance* unexpectedly froze in the icy waters off the coast of Antarctica. The ship became unsafe, a "wooden island in a sea of ice" for eight months when finally the ice began to soften. The situation became even more dangerous as the ice cracked and threatened to sink the ship as a result of the increased pressure.

Shackleton ordered his twenty-seven men off the ship and onto one of the larger ice floes, taking only their team of dogs and a few necessary supplies. I recommend that you read the story in full to appreciate the meaning of "endurance" and to see an example of crisis leadership in action, which calls for a constant revising of goals as needed. It was Shackleton's primary objective not only to save himself but all the lives of his crew. As the captain, he felt that each member of the crew was created in the divine image, like himself. And in the end, he believed that by God's grace he succeeded—a good example of strategic thinking under pressure.

I have read his story more than once. It gives me strength as I consider the challenges to social justice today compared to the dangers in the icy sea of Antarctica. Shackleton's challenges fell on followers and leaders. Yes, I do believe God is gracious, but if all hope is gone, I would second what Sir Edmund Hillary, the first person to reach the summit of Mt. Everest, said: "When you feel hope is slipping, get down on your knees and pray for a Shackleton."[5] How many of us can imagine such a prayer being uttered today bearing our name and offered as a prayer of hope? The reality is that we are all unexpected followers and leaders who may currently be afraid to be involved in a difficult situation. The consequences of our inaction may be worse than we realize. In today's changing and conflicted world, people may look to us to find a new pathway of goodwill in the midst of our human diversity.

Take the story of businessman Dan Ponder from Georgia, who several years ago received the JFK Profile in Courage award as a result of his extraordinary speech made to Georgia lawmakers on legislation to impose extra penalties for "hate crime" attacks on minorities, gays, and others. He grew up in segregated Cottonwood, Alabama; was president of his all-white fraternity at Auburn University; and was elected to the Georgia legislature as a Republican representing a conservative rural district. He never expected to be recognized by the Kennedy clan, as we can well imagine. The Profile in Courage award is given to public figures who by their example put principle ahead of political expediency.

Ponder was a quiet, laid-back kind of person who was genuine in his humility. He was probably the last person you would expect to speak out on any controversial "hate crime" legislation. He saw himself simply as a South Georgia businessman who owned a Hardee's fast-food franchise and was a well-regarded public citizen. He appeared ordinary until that day he stood to speak to the Georgia legislature on behalf of the controversial hate-crime legislation, giving a brief account of his youth in rural Cottonwood.

Ponder began his presentation by saying he was raised by Mary Ward, a young black woman whose grandmother had raised his mother:

One day when I was about 12 or 13, I was leaving for school. As I was walking out the door, she turned to kiss me goodbye. And for some reason, I turned my head. She stopped looking at me and she looked into my eyes with a look that absolutely burns in my memory right now and she said, "You didn't kiss me because I am black." At that instant, I knew that she was right. . . . I denied it. I made some lame excuse about it. But I was forced at that age to confront a small dark part of myself. I don't even know where it came from. This lady, who was devoting her whole life to me and my brother and sister, who loved me unconditionally, who had changed my diapers and fed me, and who was truly my second mother, that somehow she wasn't worthy of a goodbye kiss simply because of the color of her skin. Hate is all around us. It takes shape and form in ways that are somehow so small that we don't even recognize them to begin with, until they somehow become acceptable to us.

I have lived with the shame and memory of my betrayal of Mary Ward's love for me. I pledged to myself then and I re-pledged to myself the day I buried her that never, ever again would I look in the mirror and know that I had kept silent. Likewise, my wife and I promised to each other on the day that our oldest daughter was born that we would raise our children to be tolerant. That we would raise them to accept diversity and to celebrate it. In our home, someone's difference would never be a reason for injustice.[6]

When Rep. Ponder sat down, to his great surprise and joy he received a thunderous ovation from both sides of the political aisle, from black and white lawmakers alike. The Georgia House then reversed itself and passed the once "controversial" hate-crime bill. Don Ponder's courage was tackling issues of justice that he had once been afraid to confront. May his tribe increase over those who either "love together selfishly" or "hate together selfishly" on whatever the issue might be at the moment, to help "them" and "us" all to realize that neither side can talk about the evils of the other side without realizing we are all accountable for our actions whenever we deface the divine image in one another.

Today, colleges and universities are establishing "diversity officers" on their campuses to help create a lasting change.[7] There is a growing tide to practice racial unity in higher education in our battle against intolerance. The concern of higher education officials is to influence the values and attitudes of followers and leaders of the next generation. By improving behavior in our inner selves, we will learn to be respectful in a diverse world—and to teach others to be respectful—as we uncover our common humanity. In today's business community, likewise, there are growing numbers of social entrepreneurs and innovators who are committed to doing good as well as making a profit. By their conscience and compassion they seek to improve the quality of life, narrowing the gap between rich and poor and discovering in the process our mutual need for each other.[8]

Actually, many unexpected leaders (unknown to us) are already present in society in far greater numbers than we realize. As individuals become empowered to do more than they could themselves imagine, we will grow persons to be engaged in caring for the world as was divinely intended. The time is now and the need is great to tackle the issues of injustice, poverty, and disease that we have neglected through our ignorance and misplaced fears. We must be willing to really see as well as listen to the global neighborhood challenging us to question the status quo. We can be like the writer Anne Lamott, who began by praying for courage and discovered that "courage is merely fear that has said its prayers."[9] As Pastor John M. Buchanan of the Fourth Presbyterian Church in Chicago reminds us, "Faithful courage is not the absence of fear. It is the willingness to act, to follow, to be, in the face of fear."[10] Lamott and Buchanan both emphasize that courage is required if followers and leaders are to hear the many voices from the neighborhoods that can no longer be ignored.

BE A PLAYER/COACH

Leadership also requires the courage to face failures and unexpected tragedies encountered in organizational life. Addressing such issues may be the toughest challenges facing leaders who are called to act as caring coaches in difficult circumstances. In many respects acquiring a calm perspective is one of the most important characteristics for able leaders to acquire before their members. Assuming the role of a player/coach enables leaders to relate on all levels of the organization, helping others through their feelings of loss or self-doubt, wondering at times if they have what it takes to contribute significantly in a timely and focused way. *Webster's Dictionary* informs us that courage is the quality of mind or spirit that enables us to face difficulty, danger, pain, and so on, without fear and seen as an expression of our bravery. Courage is often witnessed in public as gutsy determination, whatever the circumstances, to lead in a calming and realistic spirit without the self-pity and gloom one often hears in the halls of an organization.

We can usually choose which attitudes and responses to demonstrate before life's challenges. We may not be able to change what seems inevitable or what has already transpired, but we can help one another sing the one song we agree on as a team, namely, to work together to make a contribution that energizes our lives. Promoting an adventuresome spirit in taking risks pulls organizations, institutions, and communities together to enhance their outreach and mission.

At this point, you may be questioning whether your own common sense is sufficient to confront today's realities. You may suddenly be faced with an unexpected challenge that increases your level of anxiety. In the midst of a sudden tragedy a positive reaction will make a difference in the world and give you a sense of accomplishment and fulfillment. There have been few times as difficult as today for families, friends, and organizations hoping to count on someone's help or loyalty when needed. Ours is a world of eroding trust, with layers of suspicion and skepticism surfacing daily. Is there anyone we can really trust anymore? This situation is unfortunate, even tragic, but it is the story of our lives today; it could even become our apocalypse.

Are our common-sense responses still sufficient to provide us with a calm perspective and hope in today's profit-and-loss environment? In other words, ours is a win/lose society; some simply refer to it as a "business-oriented society," with all its uncertainties. Unemployment is high; property values oscillate; homes are lost to foreclosure; livestock markets are threatened by pandemic diseases; and Wall Street is tarnished by scandal. To survive and prosper, our global society will demand that brave and committed individuals—as followers and as leaders—believe that their lives can make a difference in keeping human life human in this age of random killing and flickering opportunities.

In spite of some global signs of recovery, many negative indications still persist, causing doubts and raising alarming concerns. We claim to be people of hope, but our religious and nonreligious traditions are often controlled by a restrictive framework of conformity. Is our talk of a promising future simply an illusion? Are we trapped in despair? No economic victory will be easily handed to any of us. No one can promise a smooth pathway that climbs to success. To suffer in our struggles is normally the working creed that forms our identity and develops our character. We operate throughout our global society with the belief that divine destiny is behind us and will enable us to endure, whatever the odds might be against us. Perhaps such a belief may be an illusion, too. The search for meaningful answers to unanswered questions is the story of our lives around the world. Absolute certitudes may be beyond our grasp; our destiny is wrapped up in faith, not finite certitudes.

Since 9/11, Americans have begun to experience the many vulnerabilities already found in our global society; we are all edgy and eager to safeguard ourselves. The insecurity admittedly is not simply ours; it's also the world's picture of reality today. It seems we are all struggling to make sense of our fragile existence without losing our sanity in the process. We want to be realistic with ourselves and with our organizations and institutions; yet in the atmosphere of tension and distrust we are discovering how difficult and confusing the boundaries between right and wrong have become within a multicultural society.

Whether rich or poor, we seem unable to articulate the meaning of human coexistence when our dignity has been defaced and even destroyed. We have either used or abused our religious traditions to our ends, increasing the number of skeptics surrounding us. Whatever we have to say to one another no longer seems relevant nor helpful, increasing our feelings of hopelessness. This is difficult for believers in any tradition to admit. In today's world, no side seems to know how to connect meaningfully with the other, let alone put together a global peace plan that can restore our collective humanity and provide a promising future for humankind. The reality is that we continue to experience senseless bloodshed. Our wounds go unhealed in this imperfect, unforgiving world, leaving us crippled, unfulfilled, and thirsting for a better way.

If this is your understanding of present reality, then perhaps the following "paradoxical commandments" expressed by Kent M. Keith, a businessman and educational leader, will give a useful perspective and encouragement.[11] Keith says that because the world is crazy and we are not, we can find support and purpose by viewing the paradoxes of life as opportunities for service. A paradox, as we normally use the term, is an idea that is contrary to popular opinion, something that seems to contradict common sense and yet is actually true.

Keith invites us to act paradoxically (to think outside the framework of common sense) and practice an uncommon-sense wisdom that calls us to step aside from reacting as expected and to think in a contrary "outside the box" paradoxical manner, knowing that our well-being is at stake. His ten paradoxical commandments or, as I prefer to say, statements of uncommon wisdom are as follows:

1. We all have our disappointments with one another because "people are illogical, unreasonable, and self-centered." Uncommon wisdom beckons us to "love them, anyway."
2. "If you do good, people will accuse you of selfish, ulterior motives." Uncommon wisdom says, "Do good anyway."
3. "If you are successful, you will win false friends and true enemies." Uncommon wisdom calls us to "succeed anyway."
4. "The good you do today will be forgotten tomorrow." Uncommon wisdom says, "Do good anyway."
5. "Honesty and frankness make you vulnerable." Uncommon wisdom says, "Be honest and frank anyway."
6. "The biggest men and women with the biggest ideas can be shot down by the smallest men and women with the smallest minds." Uncommon wisdom says, "Think big anyway."
7. "People favor underdogs, but follow only top dogs." Uncommon wisdom calls us to "fight for a few underdogs, anyway."
8. "What you spend years building may be destroyed overnight." Uncommon wisdom says, "Build anyway."
9. "People really need help but may attack you if you do help them." Uncommon wisdom calls us to "help people, anyway."
10. "Give the world the best you have, and you'll get kicked in the teeth." Uncommon wisdom beckons us to "give the world the best you have, anyway."

I would add an eleventh uncommon wisdom that calls us to practice forgiving love regardless of the painful scars from unhealed wounds. To "forgive and forget" is actually impossible for humans to undertake, but learning to practice forgiveness without forgetting the scars of the past is the uncommon wisdom we require if we wish to keep human life human and move forward, transforming our feelings of despair into a renewing spirit that is willing to pursue the rainbow of hope and its beckoning promise.

Here we have it—an uncommon wisdom with its list of directives, leading to a more meaningful life. This paradoxical or contrarian outlook points us beyond our usual commonsense ways and invites us to take a deeper plunge into ourselves, awakening the divine image that lies listless within us. Once awakened, it will help satisfy our soul's yearning for a more promising future, one in which we are passionately engaged through our organizations, institutions, governments, businesses, and communities to make a difference that counts, lifting the quality of our lives to succeed together as we uncover one another's humanity.

Hopefully this book has encouraged readers to deepen their understanding of followership and leadership in order to have a more fulfilling life. If this can become a shared goal, we can be soul mates entrusted to build communities of faith, hope, and love as we learn each other's language and tradition. We can call ourselves "Olympic villages," acknowledging our shared diversity and competitive spirits but nevertheless willing to race in peace together, whatever the pressures and outcomes might be.

Afterword

On the Highway to the Sun

In recent years, I have spent my summer breaks speaking and writing at St. Timothy's Chapel, with its ecumenical services and music programs, located in the Pintler Mountains of Montana. This has also given our family the opportunity to make friends with Montanans and to visit Glacier and Yellowstone National Parks.

Those of you who have been to Glacier National Park know something of its majesty and beauty. After entering the grounds, we headed for the famous "Going to the Sun Road" near the Continental Divide. It was breathtaking to see the many wildflowers, tall evergreens, mountain goats, bullhorns, birds, and trout streams all in abundance. The view inspired the wish that this beauty will continue to flourish depending on how responsible we are in caring for our environment. We are all accountable for protecting and nurturing our green resources on planet earth. Each of us, when we take moments to think strategically, are embarked on a highway to the sun for good or ill, depending on our outlook and mission in life.

Yesterday's borders are increasingly obsolete symbols in our lifetime. Many of us are reaching out for that rainbow of hope as yesterday's dreams fade and today's anxieties reign. Nevertheless, generations of the future will have, I believe, a far greater universe to explore if we take more responsibility now to keep the imagination of our youth alive and well. Scientists and planners in many fields of study, however, are already anticipating both positive and negative scenarios for humankind. It depends on the conditions and choices that are made today. The future of our children, grandchildren, and great-grandchildren depends on our values and directions, which influence the actions and reactions currently transpiring in the geopolitics of our changing global society. I wonder, as I lounge with my family while visiting the MySpace Web site in the family room: Are future generations being prepared to absorb change creatively? Or are we all quietly frozen in fear and confusion, young and old alike, as we view on the screen the ascendancy of mistrust and violence in today's global society?

Sir Richard Branson, CEO of Virgin Group Ltd., who is well known for his daring business creativity, generosity, and maverick spirit, is already engaged in building Virgin Galactic, which will connect with five space hotels.[1] An increasing number of organizations—profit and nonprofit—are beginning to join Branson's example as they widen their portals of progress in a common quest to travel in space to Mars and beyond. Global travel will no longer be limited to international travel; we will see ourselves increasingly embarking on universal space travel around the sun and beyond. The rainbow of hope will extend far beyond the mountaintops and valleys, exceeding our imagination and grasp.

Organizational wisdom anticipates a larger horizon ahead—a universal highway that expands our understanding of progress, peace, and prosperity as we have envisioned it. But how visionary can we afford to be when leadership under pressure is focused primarily on one crisis or another in a world of broken relationships, mistrust, and greed? A universal highway is unlikely to become a reality until we are able to confront realistically the high cost of past errors and the shared responsibilities as we clean up the mess on our roadsides and areas of poverty around the world. How willing and ready are we to transcend issues of blame and guilt that we shower on one another without meaningful results? We spend too much energy looking backward rather than forward in our dealings with one another. Frankly, there is no safety for anyone anywhere—weapons, walls, and gated communities are not the answers that will have enduring significance. A more lasting sense of safety is found when collectively we agree to reach out as a global community with mutual trust, empowered to put in place workable (though not perfect) resolutions to thorny issues that have divided communities, nations, and families since recorded history. We need to remind ourselves constantly that we are at best imperfect persons who make imperfect decisions in an imperfect world. At least, that is my framework of human reality when I engage in serious dialogue. What's yours?

Professor Peter Drucker, the organizational guru of the past century, wisely observed that faith-based institutions premise their future hopes on the belief that divine faithfulness exists to benefit humankind. In other words, the divine will intends neither to fail nor forsake us. This is our hope at the end of the rainbow, in spite of storms and setbacks during the course of the journey. On the other hand, we humans, with our finite perspective, continue to be troubled with our worries. The prevailing fear is that we will fail God for whatever reason, not that God will fail us. In short, we maintain a twofold tension in life, namely, a strong desire to succeed on our terms and an insufficient confidence in divine faithfulness to fulfill us. Our negative attitudes motivate us to lie and cheat to reach our goals of self-interest. And in the process we deface the divine image and disrespect one another in our dealings together. In practice, we tend to be tangled up and confused in our feelings and loyalties. Where does our final allegiance lie? To whom are we accountable? And how honest have we been with ourselves?

Confessing our sins and uttering our creeds may be more a ritual than an actual entrance to the realities of our faith tradition. Every sector of today's global society confronts this issue whether we are willing to admit it to ourselves or not. The marketplace is looking for positive deeds and authentic healing that can be shared in our Facebooks. Quite frankly, we are being tested on all levels all the time regarding the integrity and wisdom of our leadership in the organization and in the community. Religious standards in every tradition finally point to ethical practices. Our results unfortunately tend to be inconsistent. That is why we ought to take time for honest prayer and forgiveness to renew our ties—divine and human.

The miracle in all this is that divine faithfulness continues to be extended to us in spite of our unfaithfulness and inconsistency. The status quo in our lives can always be challenged, and opportunities to experience forgiveness and trust await as we seek to change directions and resume lives and relationships of respect for each other's dignity and well-being—as divinely intended.

Forgiveness and trust will be more difficult on our next go-round, when we truly feel hurt and the scars are still there to remind us of those past events. We feel pain most during the course of healing when we are hurt again and the relationship is broken again. Some have even given up at this point, believing forgiveness is only a myth that's rehearsed in our religious institutions but doesn't actually square with the harsh realities of life. You may know of persons in the marketplace who have adopted this outlook, including family members. Leadership in government, education, religion, and the public square are all under pressure to have healthy organizations where trust and forgiveness are no longer in such short supply in addressing today's needy and conflicted world.

The competitive marketplace everywhere needs to regain its ethical compass for the twenty-first century. Any organization's competitive advantage lies in fulfilling its ethical responsibilities to its public at home and abroad. In this way, we will uncover a universally reliable road map for every community to succeed wherever they exist in our global society. The task of restoring an ethical road map will not be easy for any organization faced with temptations to win at any cost. And we know that organizations are under competitive pressure before their chain of suppliers around the world. Nonprofit organizations are not exempt from similar economic pressures in their efforts to do good.

We are all in need of direction and wisdom, especially when we are hit by an impending storm and discover the rainbow of hope is hidden behind the clouds. There is a feeling of despair in the air for us all. These are indeed crucial times for communities and leaders of organizations who are able by grace to pull everyone together against great odds. All of us are needed to speed the relief process as the rainbow appears in all its splendor, announcing that we are not forsaken. In today's and tomorrow's global society we must learn to succeed together. There is no safety, peace, or future otherwise.

Making mistakes in our effort to do good is inevitable. Judging sincerity accurately when under pressure is difficult, if not impossible. Leadership that counts will not judge too quickly but also will avoid making denials for oneself or the team, or, for that matter, allowing self-pity to be an excuse when we are caught in a tight situation. Ask your people to stop looking for excuses to cover up the situation; instead, maximize information and then develop another plan of action. Waiting too long for a decision may be too late. However, acting too quickly in ignorance can also be deadly. Wisdom is having the hindsight before the event to weigh the consequences that would follow the decision and to determine the direction desired. Leaders need to look ahead without being cocky.

Remember, on the highway to the sun we are all exposed to the sun's rays. Nothing is hidden, especially the very conditions that pressured us to compromise on core values, undermining the organization's mission and image. In the long run, such compromises will harm the organization. Engage in truthful encounters—they're the best sunscreen to protect yourself and members of the organization. And the best sunscreens in the marketplace are known as Forgiveness and Restitution—both to be applied with care and humility. Either can initiate the healing process after yesterday's debacle or tomorrow's unexpected disappointment.

Caring leadership never forsakes the team under trying circumstances. Organizational strength is found when we act together as an extended family, accepting each other's support and respecting the other's dignity. Human relationships may never be perfect and, in fact, will sometimes disappoint us despite our good intentions. Developing integrated teams in organizations can transform us into an extended family with a greater willingness to care, forgive, and be real as we learn to work together. The leader at the same time needs to exemplify a high standard of morale to advance the organization's mission, heralding in a variety of ways its message, services, and products.

Time itself can also be an important healing factor where broken relationships exist; we must be willing to wait for the healing process to complete its task, allowing members to reflect on the larger picture and to place themselves and issues in perspective. Rethinking our common journey can actually ignite in us a more creative outlook for the organization's rebirth.

Including a player/coach on every integrated team will help immensely to keep communication open and lively, offering fresh approaches to problem solving to benefit the organization. I suspect that Albert Einstein may have assumed this role unofficially at the Institute for Advanced Studies at Princeton. His creative suggestions, endless humor, and candor encouraged, I suspect, his cohorts to pursue fresh insights in their respective journeys to explore the universe.[2]

Leadership that builds community will also make time for special celebrations and recognition of one another's achievements in the organization. These collective gatherings can also enable members to appreciate one another's difficult moments—moments when frustrations are evident in their zigs and zags on the highway to new discoveries.[3]

Coming together socially in the organization can also establish new benchmarks of self-understanding; no doubt everyone's journey is lonely at times. To hear a word of critical appreciation that expresses trust and confidence when one is in the midst of hard work and doubts can relieve both personal and work-related tensions. After all, we need one another not only as colleagues but also as caring human beings. I suspect there are outstanding leaders in every organization who are without close friends. It may be their choice, but on the other hand, most of us, I think, find value in relationships as well as in our moments of privacy. We realize with time that every organization has individuals who might welcome a listening ear. Such moments also remind us that we need one another if we are to succeed in our totality as an organization.

In short, as leaders and as followers our common aim is to exceed our goals with humility and thankfulness, whatever the pressures might be. From experience we have observed that every significant undertaking will probably remain unfinished in our lifetime. The divine rainbow will beckon every new generation, hopefully to undertake unfinished goals for their time. Change is inevitable; we must focus on it as an opportunity, not the enemy. The leadership team must act together in their commitment to teach by example, following the ABCs of success discussed in these pages.

Yes, leadership is always under pressure. And competent and courageous leadership does matter. Furthermore, creative partnerships are necessary if organizations are to succeed in the changing marketplace of ideas, where the public ought to have the freedom of choice.

Appendix

TOPICS FOR DISCUSSION STARTERS

The following appendix items with questions can be useful as discussion starters:

Abraham Lincoln—"Meditation on the Divine Will"

Leadership Insights from Scripture

The Presidential Office: Intersecting Leadership Functions in My Experience

Challenges Facing Religious Institutions: Preparing God's People for Service

Marketplace Ethics Questionnaire

Discussion Endgame: Building a Culture of Strategic Thinking from the Beginning that Benefits Organizational Success

ABRAHAM LINCOLN

"Meditation on the Divine Will"

The will of God prevails. In great contests each party claims to act in accordance with the will of God. Both may be, and one must be wrong. God cannot be for and against the same thing at the same time. In the present civil war it is quite possible that God's purpose is something different from the purpose of either party—and yet the human instrumentalities, working just as they do, are of the best adaptations to affect His purpose. I am almost ready to say this is probably true—that God wills this contest, and wills that it shall not end yet. By His mere quiet power, on the minds of the now contestants, He could have either saved or destroyed the Union without human contest. Yet the contest began. And having begun He could give the final victory to either side any day. Yet the contest proceeds.

September 3, 1962

Question: Is Lincoln's understanding of the "Divine Will" a helpful guide today?

Note: In the last analysis, for Lincoln, God is expected to be judge for what is God's will, whatever the nature of the conflict might be. The above meditation by Lincoln on the divine will was taken from the recent book by Ronald C. White Jr., *Lincoln's Greatest Speech: The Second Inaugural* (New York: Simon & Schuster, 2002).

LEADERSHIP INSIGHTS FROM SCRIPTURE

"What do you want?" Jesus asked. She said, "Give your word that these two sons of mine will be awarded the highest place of honor in your kingdom, one at your right, one at your left hand." Jesus responded, "You have no idea what you're asking." And he said to James and John, "Are you capable of the drink I'm about to drink?" They said, "Sure, why not?" Jesus said, "Come to think of it, you are going to drink my cup. But as to awarding places of honor, that's not my business. My Father is taking care of that." When the ten others heard about this, they lost their tempers, thoroughly disgusted with the two brothers. So Jesus got them together to settle things down. He said, "You've observed how godless rulers throw their weight around, how quickly a little power goes to their heads. It's not going to be that way with you. Whoever wants to be great must be a servant. Whoever wants to be first among you must be your slave. That is what the Son of Man has done: He came to serve, not be served—then to give away his life in exchange for the many who are hostages."

(Matt. 20:21–28)

Take a good look, friends, as who you were when you got called into this life. I don't see many "the brightest and the best" among you, not many influential, not many high-society families. Isn't it obvious that God deliberately chose men and women that the culture overlooks and exploits and abuses, chose these "nobodies" to expose the hollow pretensions of the "somebodies"? That makes it quite clear that none of you can get by with blowing your own horn before God. Everything that we have—right thinking and right living, a clean slate and a fresh start—comes from God by way of Jesus Christ. That's why we have the saying, "If you're going to blow a horn, blow a trumpet for God."

(1 Cor. 1:26–31)

So, chosen by God for this new life of love . . . dress in the wardrobe God picked out for you: compassion, kindness, humility, quiet strength, discipline. Be even-tempered, content with second place, quick to forgive an offense. Forgive as quickly and completely as the Master forgave you. And regardless of what else you put on, wear love. It's your basic all-purpose garment. Never be without it.

(Col. 3:1–14)

". . . for the Spirit in you is far stronger than anything in the world."
(1 John 4:4b)

The somebodies will be nobodies and the nobodies will be somebodies.
(Matt. 19:30)

Question: What meaningful statements direct your life goals?

Note: All passages, except the last, are translated by Eugene H. Peterson in *The Message: The Bible in Contemporary Language* (Colorado Springs, CO: NavPress, 2002). The last quotation (Matt. 19:30) is translated by John Dominic Crossan.

THE PRESIDENTIAL OFFICE

Intersecting Leadership Functions in My Experience

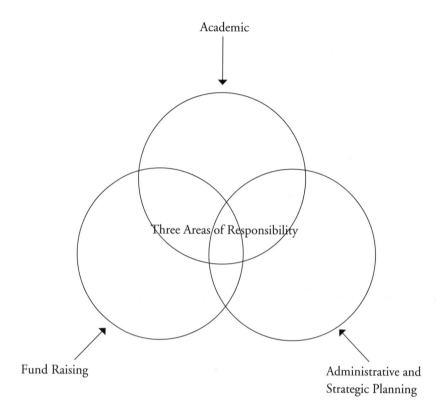

Academic

Three Areas of Responsibility

Fund Raising

Administrative and
Strategic Planning

Academic Functions

—Faculty development
—Student enrollment
—Develop innovative links on and off campus
—Encourage and nurture publications
—Strive for excellence
—Promote vigorous post-tenure and curriculum reviews
—Build intentional quality time with students
—Encourage shared faculty and student worship (chapel), Bible study, and prayer

Academic Functions (*cont.*)

—Expand continuing education offerings and outreach; enrichment program events such as:
—Metro-Urban Institute (MUE)
—World Mission Initiative (WMI)
—Center on Business, Religion and Public Life
—Kelso Bible Land Museum and Research Center
—Summer Youth Institute (SYI)
—Be a teaching president at school and with the public
—Publish articles and books periodically

Fund-Raising Functions

—Increase the endowment
—Build up the annual fund
—Win new friends to support the Seminary
—Preach in churches and speak in other public forums locally, nationally, and internationally
—Maintain sound record keeping in the Development and Business Offices
—Work with newspapers, TV/Internet, and magazines to tell the Seminary's story and enhance its public image
—Develop partnerships with grant makers
—Understand the community's needs as well as the Seminary's needs
—Develop among seminarians a spirit of pastorpreneurship as well as stewardship

Administrative and Strategic Planning Functions

—Share your visionary process with all the stakeholders of the Seminary

—Articulate clearly the role of theological education for the revitalization of churches and neighborhood

—Encourage the Seminary to expand distance education programs

—Maintain and update classrooms and library facilities

—Engage everyone associated with the Seminary, including students and alums, to fulfill their goals for excellence

—Always be aware that the Seminary is God's school, not yours

—Uphold your faithfulness before God and practice forgiveness with yourself and toward others

Question: As head of an educational organization how would you outline your responsibilities? Would colleagues, trustees, and supporters agree with your presidential responsibilities? How recently have you had a frank discussion together?

Note: For background information on how these intersecting functions of leadership unfolded in my experience, see the latest book by Donald K. McKim, *Ever a Vision: A Brief History of Pittsburgh Theological Seminary, 1959–2009* (Grand Rapids: William B. Eerdmans Publishing Co., 2009). Read the strategic development of the institution as discussed in chapter 6, pages 151–224.

It may also help to read my reflection on the changing design of theological education, described in my book, *The Ideal Seminary: Pursuing Excellence in Theological Education* (Louisville, KY: Westminster John Knox Press, 2001).

CHALLENGES FACING RELIGIOUS INSTITUTIONS

Preparing God's People for Service

"Teacher, which commandment in the law is the greatest?" He said to him, "'You shall love the Lord your God with all your heart, and with all your soul, and with all your mind.' This is the greatest and first commandment. And a second is like it: 'You shall love your neighbor as yourself.' On these two commandments hang all the law and the prophets."

(Matt. 22:36–40)

Center of Circle: Challenges Seen as Opportunities

1. Educating for leadership and change in our churches and institutions.
2. Maintaining academic freedom while being faithful to confessional traditions.
3. Clarifying issues of governance, accountability, responsibility, and communication. Who owns the seminary?
4. Witnessing to the power of forgiveness within the curriculum that is flexible. What is our unique message?
5. Making the world our classroom: discovering new ways to minister in a global, multicultural, and technological society.
6. Shifting from a predominantly "clergy" paradigm to a "people of God" paradigm: expand the horizons of theological education to a wider public.
7. Enlisting and retaining qualified seminarians and lay leaders.
8. Becoming a more intentional community of faith through worship.
9. Developing financial stability: money follows ministry and increases visibility. Do we envision seminary communities joining the circle of social entrepreneurs? What is your understanding of social entrepreneurship and social enterprise?

Questions: Theological schools and churches have been designed for academic study, spiritual discernment, and worship. Are we ready to add new programs of creative outreach with emphasis on self-supporting projects that promote social enterprise? This may be the way that profit and nonprofit organizations will increasingly express their caring spirit in a global society. We will need to develop and equip "pastorpreneurs" among clergy and lay leaders to meet the challenges of a changing world with the strategic education required for the future.

Note: The above comments and questions expand on Calian's book *The Ideal Seminary: Pursuing Excellence in Theological Education* (Louisville, KY: Westminster John Knox Press, 2001).

MARKETPLACE ETHICS QUESTIONNAIRE

1. In your experience, has the chief executive set the ethical climate?

   ___completely   ___minimally
   ___considerably   ___not at all

2. How is the ethical climate in your organization upheld?

   ___regulations
   ___trusting atmosphere
   ___rewards and punishments
   ___other

3. How do you regard your organization or business to be ethical?

   ___product is beneficial for people
   ___means of production considers well-being of employees
   ___production process does not endanger health
   ___wages are good
   ___all of these

   other _____

4. Are most codes of ethics superficial or meaningful to a business organization?

   ___mostly superficial   ___mostly meaningful

   ___if other, explain:

   _____
   _____

5. Do you think that colleges and universities should offer a course devoted entirely to business ethics?
   ___yes   ___no
   ___ethics incorporated into existing courses

6. What do you think of Vince Lombardi's famous saying "Winning may not be everything, but wanting to win is!"

   ___agree   ___agree to a large extent
   ___agree slightly   ___disagree

7. Has your company engaged in a recent event of ethical consequences of which you feel especially proud? Describe:

_____

_____

_____

_____

_____

8. When does salesmanship become bribery?

___inexpensive "giveaway" (rulers, letter openers, etc.)
___moderate "giveaway" (tickets to plays or ball games, lunches, Christmas bottle of Scotch)
___expensive gifts (vacation trips, etc.)
___other

9. How would you describe the process by which you make ethical decisions? Rank the following from 1 (most important) to 6 (least important):

___common sense
___self-interest
___requirements of the law
___company interest
___religious principles (i.e., love, justice, forgiveness, etc.)
___other (specify)

_____

_____

10. Would you suffer a career setback or other subtle management retaliation if in a specific situation you put personal standards ahead of the company expectations and the management felt that business suffered somehow because of it?

___probably   ___probably not

11. If business is a game to be won or lost, should the ethics of business be seen in terms of right and wrong strategies and not in terms of absolute standards of justice, honesty, loyalty, etc.?

___yes   ___no   ___uncertain

12. Does an ethical posture improve or impede your company's business efficiency?

___improve   ___impede
___if other, explain:

_____

_____

_____

_____

13. Does customer cheating make it difficult for you to maintain your own ethical posture?

___completely   ___substantially
___moderately   ___very little
___not at all

14. Is it possible to agree on a common standard of values in our society?

___completely possible   ___highly probable
___perhaps   ___unlikely
___impossible

15. Can you be honest, profitable, and socially responsible at the same time in your business dealings?

___yes   ___no

Explain:

_____

_____

_____

_____

_____

16. What is your view of human nature? Persons are:

___basically good   ___good most of the time
___bad most of the time   ___basically bad

17. Do you feel the present ethical consciousness of your business
    community is adequate?

    ___yes   ___no

    If no, explain:

    _____
    _____
    _____
    _____

18. Do your religious beliefs affect the way you actually do business?

    ___entirely   ___to a high degree
    ___slightly   ___not at all
    ___I do not regard myself as religious.

19. Does your company support what it says about the importance
    of product quality and customer service?

    ___yes (describe process)
    ___in a limited way
    ___ no

20. How do you understand the phrase "business is business"?

    ___anything goes   ___money talks
    ___everyone has a price   ___don't expect generosity
    ___other

21. Who on the current national scene is your personal model of an
    ethical business person? (Give person's name and organization)

    _____
    _____
    _____
    _____

22. Do you believe that an ethical code established by your company makes it stronger and more profitable?

___in all cases   ___in some cases   ___not at all

Explain:

_____

_____

_____

23. You are caught in a conflict between accepted business standards at home and prevailing practices overseas. What do you do?

___adapt to the demands of the situation
___risk the loss of business
___follow the patterns already set by your competitors
___other

24. What is your motivation to be ethical? Rank the following from 1 (most important) to 5 (least important):

___reason   ___compassion
___fear of God   ___threat of being sued
___other

25. Should educational and religious institutions do more to help clarify practical ethical issues?

___yes   ___no

Explain:

_____

_____

_____

26. What basic beliefs (convictions) guide your daily decisions?

Describe briefly your response in the space below:

_____

_____

_____

_____

DISCUSSION ENDGAME

Building a Culture of Strategic Thinking from the Beginning that Benefits Organizational Success

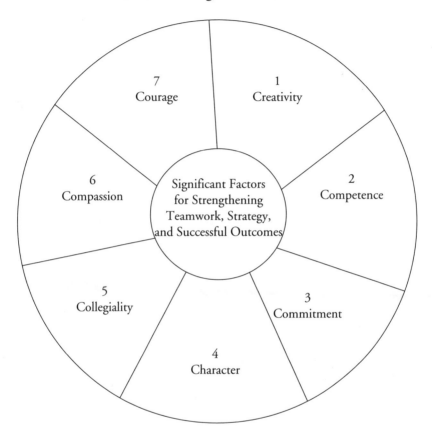

Questions:

1. In your experience, has strategic planning been an integral part of the organization's culture? If not, explain.
2. How do you think organizational strategy ensures sustainability? Should incoming CEOs initiate a strategic task force early in their leadership responsibilities? Discuss your process for organizational change.

Notes

Chapter 1: Creativity

1. See C. S. Calian, *The Gospel according to the* Wall Street Journal (Atlanta: John Knox Press, 1975).

2. "The Last Tycoon," *Time*, July 9, 2007, 33–38. See also Tim Anango, "Shaking the Bancroft Family Tree," *Fortune*, May 28, 2007, 15–16; Ken Auletta, "Promises: What Might *The Wall Street* Become If Rupert Murdoch Owned It?" *New Yorker*, June 2, 2007, 43–51; and Sarah Ellison and Matthew Karnitschnig, "Bancroft Family Agrees to $5 Billion Offer after Deal on Fees," in collaboration with Dennis K. Berman, Susan Warren, and Susan Pulliam, *Wall Street Journal*, August 1, 2007, A1, A8.

3. See Ronald A. Heifetz, "The Personal Challenge," in *Leadership without Easy Answers* (Cambridge, MA: Belknap Press, 1994), 250–76.

4. See Anthony J. Mayo and Nitin Hohria, "Zeitgeist Leadership," *Harvard Business Review*, October 2005, 15–60.

5. Alexander Schmemann, *O Death Where Is Thy Sting?* (Crestwood, NY: St. Vladimer's Press, 2003), 34–35, quoted in John Garvey, *Death and the Rest of Our Life* (Grand Rapids: Wm. B. Eerdmans Publishing Co., 2005), 72.

6. Heifetz, "The Personal Challenge," 250–76.

7. Gary L. Neilson, Bruce A. Pasternack, and Karen E. Van Nuys, "The Passive-Aggressive Organization," *Harvard Business Review*, October 2005, 84–92.

8. Ibid. 84.

9. Ibid.

10. Matthew Boyle, "Why COSTCO Is So Damn Addictive," *Fortune*, October 30, 2006, 125–30.

11. John W. Gardner, *On Leadership* (New York: Free Press, 1990), 186.

12. See Howard Gardner, *Leading Minds: An Anatomy of Leadership*, in collaboration with Emma Laskin (New York: Basic Books, 1995), 3–40.

13. Jim Collins, "The 10 Greatest CEO's of All Time," *Fortune*, July 21, 2003, 55–68. Along with Collins's discussion in *Fortune*, in addition to his well-known books, let me suggest that you will also benefit from Michael Maccoby's book *The Productive Narcissist: The Promise and Peril of Visionary Leadership* (New York: Broadway Books, 2003). I found Maccoby's survey analysis on the leader's personality helpful in my understanding of why leadership matters.

14. Collins, "The 10 Greatest CEO's." See also Peter Drucker's timeless advice to executives among profit and nonprofit organizations found in *The Essential Drucker* (New York: Harper Business, 2001) and summed up in George Andess's article "Drucker's Teachings Find Following in Asia," *Wall Street Journal*, June 18, 2008.

Chapter 2: Competence

1. Patricia Sellars, "The Recruiter," *Fortune*, November 27, 2006, 87.

2. Ibid., 89. TFA's budget in 2006 was seventy million dollars. Thirty percent comes from the government, and the rest is from private donors.

3. Peter F. Drucker, "Managing Oneself," *Harvard Business Review*, January 2005, 100–109. See also Drucker's article "What Executives Should Remember," *Harvard Business Review*, February 2006, 144–53.

4. Drucker, "Managing Oneself," 100–109.

5. John W. Gardner, *On Leadership* (New York: Free Press, 1990), 199.

6. Jeff A. Donn, "U.S. Surgeons Leave Tools in 1500 Patients in a Year, Study Finds," *Pittsburgh Post-Gazette*, January 16, 2003.

7. Thomas Neff and James Citrin, "You're in Charge. Now What?" *Fortune*, January 24, 2005, 110.

8. Ibid., 120.

9. Ronald A. Heifetz, *Leadership without Easy Answers* (Cambridge, MA: Belknap Press, 1994), 251.

10. Ibid.

11. Ibid.

12. Ibid., 268.

Chapter 3: Commitment

1. Paul Ingrassia, "The Retirement that Roared," *Wall Street Journal*, April 25, 2007 (Business Bookshelf section).

2. Lee Iacocca, *Where Have All the Leaders Gone?* (New York: Charles Scribner's Sons, 2007), 137–49.

3. Ibid., 137–38.

4. Ibid., 139. See also Mimi Swartz, *Power Failure: The Inside Story of the Collapse of ENRON,* in collaboration with Sherron Watkins (New York: Doubleday, 2003); and an earlier story on the insider-trading scandal during the 1980s that was also harmful to Wall Street, told by the Pulitzer Prize writer James B. Stewart and titled *Den of Thieves* (New York: Simon & Schuster, 1991).

5. See Donald N. Sull and Dominic Houlder, "Do Your Commitments Match Your Convictions? *Harvard Business Review*, January 2005, 82–91.

6. Michael Maccoby, "ReThinking Empowerment," *Research Technology Management* 42, no. 4 (September–October 1999): 1–3. See also Maccoby, "Under-

standing the Difference between Management and Leadership," *Research Technology Management* 43, no. 1 (January–February 2000): 57–47; and "The New Boss," *Research Technology Management* 44, no. 1 (January–February 2001): 1–4.

7. Maccoby, "ReThinking Empowerment," 3.

8. Ibid., 2.

9. This story is taken from an enlightening article by David A. Garvin and Michael A. Roberto titled "Change through Persuasion," *Harvard Business Review*, February 2005, 104–12. The article is based on a Harvard Business School case study written by Garvin and Roberto on Paul Levy's leadership at Beth Israel Deaconess Medical Center.

10. Ibid.

11. John W. Gardner, *On Leadership* (New York: Free Press, 1990), 189.

12. Dan Ciampa, "How Leaders Move," *Harvard Business Review*, January 2005, 46–47.

13. Jim Collins, "Level 5 Leadership: The Triumph of Humility and Fierce Resolve," *Harvard Business Review*, July–August, 2005, 136–47.

14. Ibid., 134.

15. Ibid., 142.

16. See the interesting discussion between top-down transformation efforts and participatory approaches to change from Harold L. Sirkin, Perry Keenan, and Alan Jackson (all authors associated with Boston Consulting Group) titled, "The Hard Side of Change Management," *Harvard Business Review*, October 2005, 109–18.

Chapter 4: Character

1. See Robert M. Galford and Anne Seibold Drapeau, *The Trusted Leader: Bringing Out the Best in Your People and Your Company* (New York: Free Press, 2002). Psychologist James Hillman, in his book *The Force of Character: And the Lasting Life* (New York: Random House, 1999), says the following about the nature of character in the context of aging: "What ages is not merely your functions and organs, but the whole of your nature, that particular person you have come to be and already were years ago. Character has been forming your face, your habits, your friendships, your peculiarities, the level of your ambition with its careers and its faults. Character influences the way you give and receive; it affects your loves and your children. It walks you home at night and can keep you long awake" (xv).

2. Howard Gardner, *Leading Minds: An Anatomy of Leadership,* in collaboration with Emma Laskin (New York: Basic Books, 1995).

3. Robert C. Solomon and Fernando Flores, *Building Trust: In Business, Politics, Relationships and Life* (New York: Oxford University Press, 2001).

4. Peter F. Drucker, "What Executives Should Remember," *Harvard Business Review*, February 2006, 152. See also John W. Gardner, *On Leadership*

(New York: Free Press, 1990). Robert T. Hurley, in his article "Managing Yourself: The Decision to Trust," *Harvard Business Review*, September 2006, 55–62, illustrates through surveys that 80 percent of Americans really don't trust corporate executives. Also approximately half of all managers don't trust their own bosses.

Chapter 5: Collegiality

1. Larry Spears, ed., *Reflections on Leadership: How Robert K. Greenleaf's Theory of Servant-Leadership Influenced Today's Top Management Thinkers* (New York: John Wiley & Sons, 1995).

2. Bill George, *Authentic Leadership: Rediscovering the Secrets to Creating Lasting Values* (San Francisco: Jossey-Bass, 2003).

3. Peter Senge, quoted in Spears, *Reflections,* 220–21.

4. Ibid., 224–25.

5. Ibid., 225.

6. Ralph Stayer, "How I Learned to Let My Workers Lead," *Harvard Business Review*, November–December 1990, 29–41.

7. Ibid., 41.

8. Ibid., 32.

9. Ibid., 33.

10. Ibid., 38.

11. Carol Hymowitz, "The Best Leaders Have Employees Who Would Follow Them Anywhere," *Wall Street Journal,* February 10, 2004.

12. Barbara Kellerman, "When Should a Leader Apologize and When Not?" *Harvard Business Review*, April 2006, 73–81. Dr. Kellerman's article is timely in light of the implied remarks by Pope Benedict XVI on Islam in a lecture at the University of Regensburg in Germany in September 2006 on "Faith and Reason." His illustration of Islam created a controversy, and he subsequently apologized a number of times publicly. Awareness of Kellerman's article by Pope Benedict XVI and his advisors might have been useful both before and after he delivered his lecture in the context of the present unrest felt by many Muslims toward the West in today's global society. For a sample of responses to the Pope's remarks, see the following news articles and opinions: "Pope Meant No Insult to Islam, Vatican Says," *USA Today,* September 15, 2006; Brett Stephens, "Pope Provocateur," *Wall Street Journal,* September 19, 2006; editorial, "Benedict the Brave," *Wall Street Journal,* September 19, 2006; and Tracy Walkimon, "Papal Gathering Aims to Staunch Islam Controversy," *Pittsburgh Post-Gazette,* September 26, 2006.

13. Kellerman, "When Should a Leader Apologize and When Not?" 74.

14. Robert W. Fuller, *Somebodies and Nobodies: Overcoming the Abuse of Rank* (Gabriola Island, BC: New Society Publishers, 2004).

Chapter 6: Compassion

1. Robert W. Fuller, *Somebodies and Nobodies: Overcoming the Abuse of Rank* (Gabriola Island, BC: New Society Publishers, 2004), 146.

2. See, for example, Max DePree, *Leadership Is an Art* (New York: Bantam Doubleday Dell Publishing Group, 1989).

3. Max DePree's comment is quoted in Bill George, *Authentic Leadership: Rediscovering the Secrets to Creating Lasting Value* (San Francisco: Jossey-Bass, 2003), 21–22.

4. Ibid.

5. Browning is quoted in ibid., 181.

6. Williams is quoted in ibid., 87.

7. Berth Jonsson quoted these words from Lao Tzu in honor of Michael Maccoby at a workshop led by Dr. Maccoby on "Leadership and Trust," March 23, 2003, in Stockholm, Sweden, under the theme "Surfing on the Wave of Learning."

8. John W. Gardner, *On Leadership* (New York: Free Press, 1990), 199.

9. See Howard Gardner, *Leading Minds: An Anatomy of Leadership,* in collaboration with Emma Laskin (New York: Basic Books, 1995), chap. 14, 267–84.

10. Peter F. Drucker, "What Makes an Effective Executive," *Harvard Business Review,* June 2004, 58–63.

11. Ibid., 62.

12. Ibid., 63.

Chapter 7: Courage

1. William Dalrymple, "Days of Rage," *New Yorker,* July 23, 2007, 33. Dalrymple has written a very informative story on Asma Jahangir of Pakistan and her current civil rights struggle with President Pervez Musharraf and his administration's lack of sufficient effort in upholding those rights and respecting the courts.

2. Ronald A. Heifetz, *Leadership without Easy Answers* (Cambridge, MA: Belknap Press, 1994), 275. See also Ronald A. Heifetz and Marty Linsky, "A Survival Guide for Leaders," *Harvard Business Review,* June 2002, 65–94; and Anthony J. Mayo and Nitin Nohoria, "Zeitgeist Leadership," *Harvard Business Review,* October 2005, 45–60.

3. William F. May, "Persuasion and Discernment: The Gifts of Leadership," *Christian Century,* March 10, 1999, 282–84. See also Douglas A. Ready, "How to Grow Great Leaders," *Harvard Business Review,* December 2004, 92–100; and William F. May, *Beleaguered Rulers: The Public Obligation of the Professional* (Louisville, KY: Westminster John Knox Press, 2001).

4. Quoted from Nancy F. Koehn, "Leadership in Crisis: Ernest Shackleton and the Epic Voyage of the Endurance" (case study, Howard Business School Publishing, June 16, 2003), 7–8.

5. Ibid.

6. Quoted from Albert R. Hunt's article "A Courageous Profile," *Wall Street Journal*, May 8, 2003, 10.

7. See Caryn Meyer Fliegler, "Leader for All," University/Business.com, February 2006, 57–61.

8. See Emily Eakin's article "How to Save the World? Treat It like a Business," *New York Times*, December 20, 2003, 19. See also David Bornstein's book *How to Change the World: Social Entrepreneurs and the Power of New Ideas* (New York: Oxford University Press, 2004) and his earlier book *The Price of a Dream: The Story of the Grameen Bank* (Chicago: University of Chicago Press, 1998) about the inspired Bangladeshi economist Muhammad Yunas, who began by making possible tiny loans to millions of poor people in his country and started a microcredit movement (his idea of a bank), encouraging social entrepreneurship among the poorest of the poor. In 2006, Yunas was awarded the Nobel Peace Prize for his ideas of thirty years ago, which founded the Grameen Bank. For a brief discussion on microfinancing, see "How to Be a Microfinancier," *Wall Street Journal*, October 21, 2006, B1. As Muhammed Yunas was getting underway, approximately at the same time (and I suspect unknown to each other), the Central Committee of the World Council of Churches had approved a new organization known as the Ecumenical Development Cooperative Society (EDCS) to launch a similar loan-lending system to assist poor communities and their citizens seeking "start-up capital" that would support a social-entrepreneurial spirit with low-interest loans to help the poorest of the poor to become self-reliant. The Grameen Bank and Oikocredit (formerly known as EDCS) are both progressing well today. We can only wonder in this Internet world of ours if, had each party known the other's unfolding vision in the beginning, their combined impact and contribution could have been even greater than it is presently. To further our understanding of the implications of entrepreneurship today, read Professor Gregory Dees' paper, "The Meaning of 'Social Entrepreneurship'" (working paper, Kauffman Center for Entrepreneurial Leadership, October 31, 1998); http://www.caseatduke.org/documents/dees_sedef.pdf. Professor Dees is the Miriam and Peter Haas Centennial Professor of Public Service at the Graduate School of Business at Stanford University. Also see *The Rise of the Social Entrepreneur* by Charles Leadbeater (formerly with the *Financial Times*), published by Demos and found online at www.demos.co.uk/publications/socialentrepreneur.

9. Anne Lamott's insightful remark is found in John M. Buchanan's sermon titled "Hopes and Fears," December 11, 2005, at Fourth Presbyterian Church, Chicago, IL, p. 9.

10. Ibid. It also seems that one of the greatest sources behind our fears stems from those who disagree with these comments in organizations and hold "power" (either real or perceived) over us. Another source of fear comes from corrupt governments that are threatened by implications from possible misappropriation of financial funds for the poor. These situations exist in many parts of our world

and call for constant protest and wisdom when one is speaking out publicly. See Claudin Rosett's helpful critique and review of Jeffrey D. Sachs's recent book *The End of Poverty* (New York: Penguin Press, 2005) in the *Wall Street Journal*, March 23, 2005. Rosett is a columnist for the *Wall Street Journal*.

11. Taken from Kent M. Keith's revised book *The Paradoxical Command-ments* (Makawao, HI: Inner Ocean Publishing, 2001), 8–9. I have revised Keith's comments while maintaining faith with the author's emphasis.

Afterword

1. Michael Specter, "Branson's Luck," *New Yorker*, May 14, 2007, 114–25.

2. John Updike, "The Valiant Swabian," *New Yorker*, April 2, 2007, 74–78.

3. See Roger Martin, "How Successful Leaders Think," *Harvard Business Review*, June 2007, 60–67; Jia Lynn Young and Gerry Useem, "Cross-Train Your Brain," *Fortune*, October 30, 2006, 135–36; Jerome Groopman, *How Doctors Think* (Boston: Houghton-Mifflin, 2007); and Roderick Gilley and Clint Kilts, "Cognitive Fitness," *Harvard Business Review*, November 2007, 53–66.

Bibliography

Arbinger Institute. *Leadership and Self- Deception: Getting Out of the Box.* San Francisco: Berrett-Koehler, 2002.

Ariely, Dan. *Predictably Irrational: The Hidden Forces that Shape Our Decisions.* New York: HarperCollins, 2008.

Badaracco, Joseph L. Jr. *Questions of Character: Illuminating the Heart of Leadership through Literature.* Boston: Harvard Business School Press, 2006.

Baron, David. *Moses on Management: 50 Leadership Lessons from the Greatest Manager of All Times.* New York: Pocketbooks, 1999.

Bennis, Warren. *On Becoming a Leader.* New York: Addison-Wesley Publishing Co., 1989.

———. *Why Leaders Can't Lead: The Unconscious Conspiracy Continues.* San Francisco: Jossey-Bass, 1990.

Berry, Wendell. *What Are People For?* San Francisco: North Park Press, 1990.

Blanchard, Ken, and Phil Hodges. *The Servant Leader: Transforming Your Heart, Head, Hands & Habits.* Nashville: Thomas Nelson, 2003.

Blanchard, Ken, and Marc Muchnick. *The Leadership Pill: The Missing Ingredient in Motivating People Today.* New York: Free Press, 2003.

Bornstein, David. *How to Change the World: Social Entrepreneurs and the Power of New Ideas.* New York: Oxford University Press, 2004.

Burns, James MacGregor. *Leadership.* New York: HarperCollins, 1978.

Calian, Carnegie Samuel. *The Gospel according to the* Wall Street Journal. Atlanta: John Knox Press, 1975.

———. *The Ideal Seminary: Pursuing Excellence in Theological Education.* Louisville, KY: Westminster John Knox Press, 2002.

———. *Today's Pastor in Tomorrow's World.* New York: Hawthorn Books, 1977.

———. *Where's the Passion for Excellence in the Church?* Wilton, CT: Morehouse Publishing Co., 1989.

Campbell, Thomas C., and Gary B. Reierson. *The Gift of Administration: Theological Bases for Ministry.* Philadelphia: Westminster Press, 1981.

Coffee, John C. *Gatekeepers: The Professions and Corporate Governance.* New York: Oxford University Press, 2006.

Coles, Robert. *Lives of Moral Leadership: Men and Women Who Have Made a Difference.* New York: Random House, 2000.

Collins, James, *Good to Great: Some Companies Make the Leap and Others Don't*. New York: Harper Business, 2001.

———. *How the Mighty Fall: And Why Some Companies Never Give In*. New York: HarpersCollins, 2009.

DePree, Max. *Leadership Is an Art*. New York: Bantam Doubleday Dell Publishing Group, 1989.

Elkington, John, and Pamela Hartigan. *The Power of Unreasonable People: How Social Entrepreneurs Create Markets that Change the World*. Boston: Harvard University Press, 2008.

Feiner, Michael. *The Feiner Points of Leadership: The Fifty Basic Laws that Will Make People Want to Perform Better for You*. New York: Warner Business Books, 2004.

Foster, Charles R., Lisa E. Dahill, Lawrence A. Golemon, and Barbara Wang Tolentino. *Educating Clergy: Teaching Practices and Pastoral Imagination*. San Francisco: Jossey-Bass, 2006.

Friedman, Mac. *Encore: Finding Work that Matters in the Second Half of Life*. New York: PublicAffairs, 2007.

Friedman, Thomas L. *The World Is Flat: A Brief History of the Twenty-First Century*. New York: Farrar, Straus, & Giroux, 2005.

Founding Members. *Globally Responsible Leadership: A Call for Engagement*. Brussels: European Foundation for Management Development (EFMD), 2005.

Fuller, Robert W. *Somebodies and Nobodies: Overcoming the Abuse of Rank*. Gabriola Island, BC: New Society Publishers, 2004.

Galford, Robert, and Anne Seibold Drapeau. *The Trusted Leader: Bringing Out the Best in Your People and Your Company*. New York: Free Press, 2002.

Gardner, Howard. *Five Minds for the Future*. Boston: Harvard Business School Press, 2006.

———. *Leading Minds: An Anatomy of Leadership*. In collaboration with Emma Laskin. New York: Basic Books, 1995.

Gardner, Howard, Mihaly Csikszentmihalyi, and William Damon. *Good Work: When Excellence and Ethics Meet*. New York: Basic Books, 2001.

Gardner, John W. *On Leadership*. New York: Free Press, 1990.

Gasparino, Charles. *King of the Club: Richard Grasso and the Survival of the New York Stock Exchange*. New York: HarperCollins, 2007.

George, Bill (William W.). *Authentic Leadership: Rediscovering the Secrets to Creating Lasting Value*. San Francisco: Jossey-Bass, 2003.

Giuliani, Rudolph W. *Leadership*. New York: Hyperion, 2002.

Gladwell, Malcolm. *Blink: The Power of Thinking without Thinking*. New York: Little, Brown & Co., 2005.

———. *Outliers: The Story of Success*. New York: Little, Brown & Co., 2008.

———. *The Tipping Point: How Little Things Make a Big Difference*. New York: Little, Brown & Co., 2000.

Goffee, Rob, and James Gareth. *Why Should Anyone Be Led by You?* Boston: Harvard Business School Press, 2006.

Gryskiewicz, Stanley S., ed. *Discovering Creativity.* Greensboro, NC: Center for Creative Leadership, 1993.

Heifetz, Ronald A. *Leadership without Easy Answers.* Cambridge, MA: Belknap Press, 1994.

Heifetz, Ronald A., and Marty Linsky. *Leadership on the Line: Staying Alive through the Dangers of Leading.* Boston: Harvard Business School Press, 2002.

Hillman, James. *The Force of Character: And the Lasting Life.* New York: Random House, 1999.

Hooker, John. *Working across Cultures.* Stanford, CA: Stanford University Press, 2003.

Iacocca, Lee. *Where Have All the Leaders Gone?* New York: Charles Scribner's Sons, 2007.

Illich, Ivan, Irving Kenneth Zola, John McKnight, Jonathon Caplan, and Harley Shaiken. *Disabling Professions.* London: Redwood Burn, 1977.

Janjigian, Vahan. *Even Buffett Isn't Perfect: What You Can—and Can't—Learn from the World's Greatest Investor.* New York: Portfolio, 2008.

Jones, Laurie Beth. *Jesus CEO: Using Ancient Wisdom for Visionary Leadership.* New York: Hyperion, 1995.

Kegan, Robert, and Lisa Laskow Lahey. *How the Way We Talk Can Change the Way We Work: Seven Languages for Transformation.* San Francisco: Jossey-Bass, 2001.

Kellerman. Barbara. *Followership: How Followers Are Creating Change and Changing Leaders.* Boston: Harvard Business School Press, 2008.

Kelley, Robert. *The Power of Followership: How to Create Leaders People Want to Follow and Followers Who Lead Themselves.* New York: Doubleday Currency, 1992.

Lorsch, Jay W., and Thomas J. Tierney. *Aligning the Stars: How to Succeed When Professionals Drive Results.* Boston: Harvard Business School Press, 2002.

Maccoby, Michael. *The Leader: A New Face for American Management.* New York: Simon & Schuster, 1981.

———. *The Leaders We Need: And What Makes Us Follow.* Boston: Harvard Business School Press, 2007.

———. *The Productive Narcissist: The Promise and Peril of Visionary Leadership.* New York: Broadway Books, 2003.

May, William F. *Beleaguered Rulers: The Public Obligation of the Professional.* Louisville, KY: Westminster John Knox Press, 2001.

McKim, Donald K. *Ever a Vision: A Brief History of Pittsburgh Theological Seminary, 1959–2009.* Grand Rapids: William B. Eerdmans Publishing Co., 2009.

Micklethwait, John, and Adrian Woolridge. *God Is Back: How the Global Revival of Faith Is Changing the World.* New York: Penguin Press, 2009.

Miller, Arthur. *Death of a Salesman.* New York: Viking Press, 1950.

Morris, Thomas V. *If Harry Potter Ran General Electric: Leadership Wisdom from the World of Wizards*. New York: Doubleday, 2006.

Neff, Thomas J., and James M. Citrin. *You're in Charge—Now What? The Eight-Point Plan*. New York: Crown Business, 2005.

Nicholls, Alex, ed. *Social Entrepreneurship: New Models of Sustainable Change*. New York: Oxford University Press, 2006.

O'Toole, James. *Creating the Good Life*. Los Angeles: Rodale Press, 2005.

Pauchant, Theirry, ed. *Ethics and Spirituality at Work: Hopes and Pitfalls of the Search for Meaning in Organizations*. New York: Quorum Books, 2002.

Porras, Jerry, Stewart Emery, and Mark Thompson. *Success Built to Last: Creating a Life that Matters*. Upper Saddle River, NJ: Wharton School Publishing, 2007.

Rothkopf, David. *Superclass: The Global Power Elite and the World They Are Making*. New York: Farrar, Strauss & Giroux, 2008.

Safire, William, and Leonard Safir. *Leadership: A Treasury of Great Quotations for Everybody Who Aspires to Succeed as a Leader*. New York: Simon & Schuster, 1990.

Senge, Peter, M. *The Fifth Discipline: The Art and Practice of the Learning Organization*. New York: Doubleday, 1990.

Shore, Bill. *Revolution of the Heart*. New York: Riverhead Books, 1995.

Solomon, Robert C., and Fernando Flores. *Building Trust in Business, Politics, Relationships and Life*. New York: Oxford University Press, 2001.

Spears, Larry C. *Reflections on Leadership: How Robert K. Greenleaf's Theory of Servant-Leadership Influenced Today's Top Management Thinkers*. New York: John Wiley & Sons, 1995.

Swartz, Mimi. *Power Failure: The Inside Story of the Collapse of ENRON*. In collaboration with Sherron Watkins. New York: Doubleday, 2003.

Welch, Jack. *Winning*. In collaboration with Suzy Welch. New York: Harper Collins, 2005.

Wheatley, Margaret J. *Leadership and the New Science: Learning about Organizations from an Orderly Universe*. San Francisco: Berrett-Koehler, 1994.

Wheelis, Allen. *How People Change*. New York: Harper & Row, 1973.

White, Ronald C. Jr. *The Eloquent President: A Portrait of Lincoln through His Words*. New York: Random House, 2005.

Wooden, John. *My Personal Best: Life Lessons from an All-American Journey*. In collaboration with Steve Jamison. New York: McGraw-Hill, 2004.

Yunus, Muhammad, and Karl Weber. *Creating a World without Poverty: Social Business and the Future of Capitalism*. New York: PublicAffairs, 2007.

Zakaria, Fareed. *The Post-American World*. New York: W.W. Norton & Co., 2008.

About the Author

Carnegie Samuel Calian was awarded emeritus status in 2006 following twenty-five years of service as president and professor of theology at Pittsburgh Theological Seminary, a graduate school of professional education associated with the Presbyterian Church (U.S.A.). He has earned degrees from Occidental College (BA in philosophy) and Princeton Theological Seminary (BD in Divinity) and a doctorate in theology (DTheol) magna cum laude from the University of Basel, Switzerland. In addition he received a certificate from the Advanced Management Program (AMP) at Harvard Business School and was later invited as summer visiting scholar at Stanford University Graduate School of Business. He has also received five honorary doctorates from colleges and universities in the United States and Europe.

He has been associated with Juanita College, the University of Dubuque Theological Seminary, Oxford University's Harris Manchester College, and Carnegie Mellon University. He is presently visiting professor at the Katz Graduate School of Business at the University of Pittsburgh. In 2005, he was honored as distinguished alumnus of the year at Occidental College and Princeton Theological Seminary.

The Spirit-Driven Leader is his twelfth book. He has also published over two-hundred-plus articles in professional journals and newspapers. He is married to Doris Zobian Calian, a former research chemist and graduate of the University of Pennsylvania. They have three children and ten grandchildren.